Decoding the New Consumer Mind

Decoding the New Consumer Mind

How and Why We Shop and Buy

Kit Yarrow

Foreword by Paco Underhill

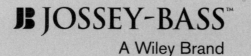

JOSSEY-BASS™

A Wiley Brand

Published by Jossey-Bass
A Wiley Brand
One Montgomery Street, Suite 1200, San Francisco, CA 94104-4594
www.josseybass.com

Jossey-Bass books and products are available through most bookstores. To contact Jossey-Bass directly call our Customer Care Department within the U.S. at 800-956-7739, outside the U.S. at 317-572-3986, or fax 317-572-4002.

Wiley publishes in a variety of print and electronic formats and by print-on-demand. Some material included with standard print versions of this book may not be included in e-books or in print-on-demand. If this book refers to media such as a CD or DVD that is not included in the version you purchased, you may download this material at http://booksupport.wiley.com. For more information about Wiley products, visit www.wiley.com.

Cataloging-in-Publication data on file with the Library of Congress.

ISBN 978-1-118-64768-4 (cloth); 978-1-118-85958-2 (ebk); 978-1-118-85931-5 (ebk)

Printed in the United States of America
FIRST EDITION
HB Printing   10 9 8 7 6 5 4 3 2 1

To my heartthrob and my hero, Russ

Contents

Foreword

Within the first few minutes of meeting Kit, you would never guess who she is and what she does. You would just feel comfortable, and that's part of how she uncovers shocking realities. Whether at a White House dinner or hanging out at her local hair salon, she has a passion for trying to make sense of the world, the people in it, and the mysteries of psychology and buying behavior. Mostly, Kit just knows.

Kit is a psychologist and professor who lectures to students and professional audiences all over the world. Her work combines academic knowledge and practical wisdom, and what makes her a good researcher is her compassion. Social science is based on emotion, and social scientists understand that truth can be transitory, unlike other fields such as physics, where reality is based on math. Kit's quest for order is about both the knowledge and the person, and she is good listener.

In the world of shopping, *Decoding the New Consumer Mind* will make waves. This important book explains it all, uncovering where we are going and showing how individuals and companies can advance their offerings as well as their bottom lines. On the heels of her first book, *Gen BuY,* Kit takes us deeper into the world of contemporary consumption—why it matters and who can benefit. The retail landscape is going to change more in the next five years than it has in the previous fifty. The nature of competition has changed drastically, and this book explains how merchants and marketers, who are struggling to keep up with the new world order, can leap forward if they have the correct tools.

The digital revolution, combined with the threat of downward mobility across the First World, is accelerating this evolution. While some of us are doing just fine, a frighteningly high percentage of Americans have been marginalized as wages have stagnated, costs are increasing, and we are forced to save where we can. We can divide our society by those who have climbed the house wall and those who are struggling. At age sixty-one, I could not afford to buy the home I now live in if I had to buy it today.

In 2014, we also have intruders in our wallets, and being connected via the web, smartphones, and other technological platforms has joined Maslow's Hierarchy of Needs. We'll feed our kids generic pasta and abandon our cars before we stop paying our mobile phone bills. Moreover, so many of our identities and emotional structures are in transition. According to census data, fewer than a quarter of American households have a mother, father, and dependent child, and the number of households where the female is the dominant breadwinner is rising.

We know that collecting data in the twenty-first century is easy. Figuring out what it means is the tough part. *Decoding the New Consumer Mind* draws on an enormous amount of thought and analysis. I am flabbergasted at the range of studies, books, and white papers that Kit cites, not to mention her own research. In an old-fashioned world, I can see her at the dining room table sorting index cards like a graduate student writing her thesis, but I am sure she has a better way. This volume is evidence of it.

Paco Underhill
CEO, Envirosell, and author,
Why We Buy

Introduction

Janine is a thirty-five-year-old high school teacher from Atlanta, and she just purchased a pair of jeans that she's unlikely to wear. If Janine's pattern holds true, they'll sit on her "jeans shelf" for a few months until they assume their final resting place: a box under her bed along with another pair of jeans, black dress slacks, a floral bustier, and a stretchy black blazer—all unworn and all still too small for Janine. A year from now they'll be resurrected and, along with the other unworn goodies, sold on eBay for a fraction of what Janine paid.

Janine isn't the first woman to buy something for a future weight—that's been a constant throughout the history of modern shopping. What's different is nearly everything about why Janine chose that particular pair of jeans; how and when she bought them; her relationship with the retailer that sold them to her; and what she'll do with those jeans in a year.

The way Janine shops today is radically different from how she shopped a decade—or even a year—ago. And that's true of most consumers. The biggest merger in the history of advertising was fueled in part by what Publicis CEO Maurice Levy described as "profound changes in consumer behavior."[1]

Janine is one of the thousands of consumers I've interviewed in the past fifteen years, and one of hundreds whom I interviewed specifically for this book. I snooped around her house, tagged along on a shopping trip, and talked with her about her life, fears, relationships—and favorite purchases.

Interviewing consumers is part of what I do as a consumer psychologist. And by that I mean a psychologist who studies why and how people shop and buy—not a therapist for shoppers. I hope my work is helpful to consumers, but my primary focus is to explain the deep motivations of consumers and emerging consumption trends to marketers so that they can better meet consumer needs and be successful.

When I talk with consumers, my goal is to understand, not judge. This respect and empathy, coupled with my training in clinical psychology, help people open up to me.

My training also allows me to make sense of what I see and hear. This comes not only from a clinical understanding of the hearts and minds of the people I interview but also through my experience as a researcher and scholar.

Psychologically informed insights are rewarding in their own right, but they're more meaningful when they're translated into information marketers can use. My experience conducting consumer research for companies as diverse as Del Monte and General Electric, and the scores of speeches I've given to marketers have laid the foundation for understanding what marketers need to know about consumers to offer better experiences and products— and consequently be more profitable companies.

Psychological insights about how, when, and why people shop and buy are the backbone of this book. These insights extend beyond consumer behavior to the place marketers need to be today: into the deeply psychological and often unconscious relationships and responses people have to products, retailers, marketing communications, and brands. The findings in this book were acquired through hundreds of consumer interviews, ethnographies, and shop-alongs, and validated and enhanced by academic and neurological research, marketing studies, and interviews with experts.

THE NEW AMERICAN CONSUMER

Janine's story demonstrates a few of the ways that the three socio-cultural shifts you'll read about in this book—technological, social, and emotional changes—now influence consumers.

Janine knows she can sell unwanted clothing on eBay, and she uses that knowledge to rationalize buying things like too-small jeans. She's not alone. Over three-quarters of women consider the resale value of what they're purchasing before they buy.[2] Consumers' vastly expanded ability to resell merchandise is one of the many ways the Internet has facilitated consumer power and reshaped buying behaviors.

In the last few years, recession-inspired discounting has super-charged the bargain expectations of consumers—and also decreased their ability to decipher the intrinsic value of merchandise. Macy's multiple promotions are like catnip to Janine. She becomes ultra-focused on the money she's saving and loses sight of what she's spending. Janine half-jokingly said, "By the time I factor in my discounts, it's like they're paying me to buy the stuff!"

Many retailers think that bargain shoppers are singularly focused on saving money. But from the consumer perspective, I've found that bargains work because they are an assurance of value, capture consumers' attention, activate their fear of missing out, and are a way to "win" against other consumers—and against retailers.

Janine shops on her smartphone during breaks at school, though she rarely makes purchases from work. Her pattern is to put the merchandise she's considering into retailer carts. She then keeps tabs so that she can snap up her finds quickly when they're reduced. The floral bustier that's under her bed right now was acquired in this manner. Janine feels victorious when her method works. Variations on this technique abound, and it's just one way that mobile technology has shaken up the marketplace. Smartphone ubiquity suits and drives the decreasing attention spans of consumers and facilitates the attentiveness necessary for what I call "competitive sport shopping."

At home, Janine often mindlessly flips though dozens of pages of online merchandise while she's watching television with her boyfriend. "It's soothing," she comments. Janine does this more when she feels anxious or disrespected—something that's increased in the past year. The most powerful triggers for Janine are work conflicts and (ironically) money stressors.

Janine isn't just shopping for jeans. Like many consumers, she's shopping for a sense of control, a distraction from anxiety, and a feeling of mastery and competence. And, like many consumers, both her anxiety level and her time and money spent online shopping have increased in the past few years.

Shopping is never exclusively about buying things we need. Social and cultural considerations have always influenced how we shop and what we buy, and especially how we use products to connect and communicate with others. It's no surprise then that a decade of especially swift and stunning sociocultural changes would have a profound effect on how and why people shop and buy.

In this book, we'll see how three fast-developing sociocultural shifts, each reinforced by the others, have transformed consumers over the last decade. As a result, consumers approach the marketplace with a different psychology. From what drives their cravings to how they shop and what they buy—this new consumer psychology demands change from marketers and retailers. The past is no longer prologue: what's been done before won't work today. And to complicate matters further, today's accelerated pace of change means that marketers have less time to get ready—they need to *be* ready. The ability to cut down the lag time between change and adaptation is a genuine competitive advantage in today's fast-paced world.

That's what I hope this book will give you: a readiness and agility in responding to change, informed by a deep understanding of the desires, motivations, habits, and buying triggers of today's new consumer. Insight into the psychology of customers is the foundation of both authentic, adaptable strategies and accelerated tactical decision making. It frees marketers from the tyranny of chasing after copycat tactics.

THREE CULTURAL SHIFTS AND FOUR MARKETING STRATEGIES TO MEET THEM

In a marketplace flooded with solutions, the particular products and brands that consumers choose will be selected because they satisfy and address a new consumer psychology. Knowing and understanding that psychology allows marketers the opportunity to more accurately predict and anticipate strategies and tactics that will resonate. In a different era of marketing, we could simply ask consumers what they liked, needed, or wanted. There are several reasons why that approach is less effective today, including

- *Lust for the new.* Consumers are eager to be delighted by the next thing and don't necessarily know what they need or want until you show them. That's not true just for technology but also for fashion, food, cars, and most of the products people buy.
- *Attention deficit.* Today's less-articulate, less-attentive consumer is also a less reliable subject in traditional research forums such as focus groups.
- *Strong emotional drivers.* Consumers' deep emotional needs are more likely to drive their purchase decisions, and these kinds of needs are something consumers have always had more difficulty articulating.

Part One of this book describes the three major sociocultural shifts that are contributing to radical changes in consumer psychology, and reflects on what these changes mean for marketers. These chapters are a deep (and sometimes dark) dive into the psychology of today's consumers, but in the end, marketers will emerge with the insights they need to build better strategies.

Rewired Brains. Because of our extensive use of technology, our brains are adapting so that we literally think differently than we did a decade ago. Our use of technology has also changed our relationships and created a whole new set of emotional needs. The cognitive and emotional shifts that result from our use of technology have permeated every aspect of our lives and consequently every aspect of how and why we shop and buy.

Isolation and Individualism. We are more guarded and self-protective today because we have less in common with others and trust institutions less. Technology-aided communication is a quantity-over-quality way of connecting that emphasizes superficiality and separateness—despite the ubiquity of social media. The net result is a sense of isolation and a more "me"-centric society.

Intensified Emotions. Research shows that although we're still optimists by nature, we're all a bit are crankier, edgier, and more anxious today. We therefore approach the marketplace with more emotionality—which means we'll process information and make decisions in different ways.

Part Two presents four essential marketing strategies that tap directly into the new consumer psychology created by these shifts.

Technovation. In a few short years, we've gone from chat rooms to Facebook, from 32-bit video games to lifelike immersive play, and from $1,000 mobile phone "bricks" to $100 four-ounce smartphones. Awe-inspiring technology that's so intimately entwined with our lives has made "new" the most coveted of brand characteristics. Companies that incorporate technology and innovation bask in the glow of "new." I've found that consumers view these companies as smarter and cooler, feel that they are trying harder to meet their (the consumer's) needs, and think their products are superior. Unless it's retro chic, "tried and true" is simply tired and old to today's consumers. Not every product has an intrinsic technological component, but every product can still use technology to appear fresh. Brands that enhance their image through technological platforms like apps, YouTube, and social media simply feel more relevant and alive to consumers. I call this injection of technology and innovation "technovation."

The concept of technovation also includes behind-the-scenes moves like the use of big data and the tailoring of organizational structures to reflect how consumers view their online and offline lives as one seamless whole.

The Real Deal. Fewer than three in ten Americans say that corporate America's reputation is positive.[3] In the minds of consumers, businesses have become the antithesis of humanity. The key to regaining the trust of wary consumers is to get real. Humanized, authentic brands that act transparently and live up to their images are beloved. Despite feeling burned, consumers still crave positive relationships with brands. Now perhaps more than ever, they want to be able to relax their guard and buy and love products without vigilance—and the brands that offer them that security have a competitive advantage.

Involvement. Today's individualistic consumer is more responsive to marketers that appear to honor, admire, and serve them. Gone are the days of "aspirational marketing" when the brand was king and consumers flocked to own a piece of something they admired. The consumer wants to be the star—and in a very personal way. The secret to cool is to make your customers feel cool—and smart for choosing your brand. The appreciated customer is one who's invited to participate. Successful companies seek the customers' opinions, offer them activities and contests, and reward their involvement.

Further, today's more emotional shopper more frequently makes decisions using mental shortcuts, rationalizes purchasing decisions more frequently, and gets frustrated more easily. Consequently, how a brand or retailer behaves and engages them is more persuasive than what it says. As we'll see in Chapter Six, the "four C's" of involving consumers with your brand are champions, customization, crowdsourcing, and contests.

Intensity. It takes *more, faster, harder, better* to break through to our technology-juiced, hyperstimulated brains. Everything has to be ramped up a bit to get attention and inspire action. Online shopping has literally put a world of options at our fingertips. With so much to choose from and no constraints on where and when to purchase, today's shopper needs a jolt of emotional intensity to pull the trigger on a purchase. Removing interference and noise—such as product complexity, confusing processes, or waiting—is another aspect of a more intense shopping experience.

•••

Each cultural shift and marketing strategy you'll encounter in this book is illustrated by examples of tactics that work, and is brought to life by the voices and stories of consumers such as Janine.

Before we begin, I'll just say a word about data. We've entered an era of data fascination. Our new love, big data (and little data too), is intoxicating because it can offer an illusion of insight and a fake sense of control in an unpredictable, overwhelming business environment. The problem is that data predict the future by analyzing the past. Given today's rapid pace of change, it's a giant risk to assume a continuation of the past.

Besides, as every great marketer knows, information is superficial and far inferior to knowledge. Data are simply tools. And although I use plenty of them in this book for illustration and support, I hope that what you leave with is a deeper, more useful knowledge of today's American consumer.

PART ONE

The New Consumer Mind

1

Rewired Brains

Technology: it's not what we do with it, but what
it's doing to us.

Sara, a waitress and San Francisco State University undergraduate
student, alternates between Neuro Sleep and 5-Hour Energy shots
to achieve just the right amount of stimulation for any given moment.
"I need something during the day. But it's hard to fall asleep after I've
been waitressing." Sara says that most of her friends also alternate
between energy products and sleep aids to help them navigate "too
much to do." And they're not alone. For a growing number of people,
"listening to your body" is only for the pharmaceutically challenged.
In 2012, sales of energy drinks grew 19 percent from 2011.[1] And
sleep-inducing products like teas, supplements, botanicals, tongue
strips, and bath salts have grown 8.8 percent annually since 2008.[2]

Sleep management is obviously a problem, but counting sheep
is so passé. Today, the marketplace is where people turn for solutions. Whether it's a supplement or an app (yes, there's an app for
that—2,938 in the iTunes store), the shift from sheep counting to
sleep supplements reflects our newfound trust in innovation and
our insistence on quick fixes—two of the many ways that our relationship with technology has changed our psychology, which has
in turn changed how we shop and what we buy.

TECHNOLOGY AND CONSUMER BEHAVIOR

In 1993, the word "web" was more likely to have been associated with a spider than something we use every day for work, entertainment, communication, and shopping. In 1995, the word "Amazon" might have conjured up thoughts of a river or a robust woman, but not the second-largest retailer in the world—which is what Wendy Liebmann, CEO of WSL Strategic, predicts Amazon.com will be by 2016.[3] And in just over thirty years, we've gone from pay phones and home phones to smartphones that are no longer simply talking devices—they're what Resource CEO Kelly Mooney insightfully describes as "weapons of personal empowerment."[4]

- The average American household has six Internet connected devices.[a]
- By 2017, the average CMO will spend more on IT than the average CIO.[b]
- More than one-third of marriages between 2005 and 2012 began online.[c]
- In 2004, YouTube didn't exist. Today, one hundred hours of video are uploaded every minute of every day, and over a billion unique users visit YouTube every month.[d]

Although parents, psychologists, politicians, philosophers, scientists, and educators hotly debate whether technology and the Internet are good or bad for us, there's one thing that cheerleaders, hand-wringers, and everyone between agrees on: technology *has* changed us. And the influence of technology will only increase. Two-thirds of kids between seven and thirteen would rather have technology, such as a tablet, to play with than a toy.[5]

I'll explain in this chapter how in a relatively short period of time—so fast that we've barely had time to register the impact—the pervasiveness of technology in our lives has affected every aspect of being human: how we think and make decisions, how we feel, what we crave, and how we relate to others.

Obviously this is of great importance to marketers. After all, people buy to elevate their emotional state, whether by removing a negative, satisfying aspirations, or gaining a positive. They are solving and improving both practical and emotional problems and situations. And even purely practical purchases will be strongly influenced by an emotional overlay of things like self-identity, belonging, obligation, or boredom. Technology has created a new set of "problems" and emotional needs, new ways of acquiring perceptions of products and brands, and new ways of interacting with the marketplace. The hunt for happiness has evolved.

There is immense pressure on marketers to conceptualize how to use the flood of new technology and platforms to engage with consumers. Although new platforms provide important tactical solutions in connecting with today's consumer, I believe that the bigger opportunity is in driving new strategies that take their cue from how technology has changed the consumer.

Today's frenzied pace of innovation renders "now" an increasingly untrustworthy predictor of what consumers will want tomorrow. Although meaningful insights (as well as tactical solutions) can be culled from market and technology trends, marketers with a deeper, empathic understanding of the psychology of consumers can build high-impact, sustained strategies swiftly and with confidence. It's a significant opportunity for the marketers who get it, and it's what I'll focus on in this chapter.

FIVE PSYCHOLOGICAL SHIFTS

Five key psychological shifts catalyzed by our use of technology are of particular importance to how, when, and why people shop and buy. These psychological shifts are also affected by the other two major sociocultural shifts we'll explore: our elevated levels of emotionality and an increased sense of isolation. Each of the three contributes to the effects of the others in a dynamic, mutually reinforcing manner. Our use of technology has changed our psychology in these ways:

1. Innovation optimism
2. Consumer empowerment
3. Faster ways of thinking
4. Symbol power
5. New ways of connecting

Innovation Optimism

Today we're all early adopters. Once hesitant, consumers have become eager to try new products. The usefulness, ubiquity, and intimacy of technology have transformed innovation-wary consumers into optimists.

Brenda, for example, has a problem with navigation. "I can get lost in a closet, I swear. I have no sense of direction. I remember clearly why I bought my first cellphone. I was driving around lost and late for a date. I couldn't find a pay phone, and I couldn't even find where I was on a map. I got there, but I was like an hour late. I was stressed and anxious, and my boyfriend was mad. That was only maybe fifteen years ago. What a different life I have—not just navi and cellphone, but it's hard to believe in my life I used a typewriter. It's all so much easier and better now."

The deep intimacy we have with our technology—phones that rest on our nightstands and computers that we interact with more than people—is unlike any relationship we've had with products in the past. And continuous brilliant advances in technology, coupled with the power of social media to champion new products, have created a trust in "new" unlike anything we've seen before.

Products of all sorts, not just technology, have benefited. In the past, most consumers would have fallen into the "wait and see" category of shoppers. Today, like Brenda, nearly everyone is less suspicious and more willing to try unfamiliar products.

I found my job, my apartment, and my boyfriend online.
—Jemmie, 26

In fact, eagerness and even insistence might better describe many consumers' view of innovation. This is particularly true of those younger than thirty-three, the first generations to grow up in a digital world. They have high expectations, and, like Sara, who turns to the marketplace for sleep solutions, they want quick fixes to their problems, and they view innovation as the hallmark of excellence in product design and communication.

Sara's faith in the power of purchases to quickly fix problems is due, in part, to the brilliant innovation she's witnessed in the technology that's fundamental to her life. Every new generation of computer or cellphone is proof that new is better, faster, and hipper.

The intersection of innovation and the demand for immediate solutions is highlighted by a new phenomenon the *New York Times* called "smartphone shrinks."[6] Apps like iStress, MoodKit, Fix a Fight, and Unstuck use algorithms to tackle the kinds of problems a therapist might have been called on to help with in the past. The popularity and prevalence of these apps are yet another indication of our quest for the quick fix—a direct result of our belief in the power of innovation and of the impatience we've developed through our use of technology.

New? Bring It ON

Consumer cravings for "new" are bolstered through the consumer championship and trust building of social media, rating, and review sites. Products can go from introduction to popularity at an unprecedented rate through the reach and reassurance provided by social media. The ability of the Internet to provide a platform, voice, and marketplace for new companies and entrepreneurs has facilitated the rise of fresh, nimble brands that excite consumers and satisfy their craving for "new." The growing clout of new brands is reflected in the annual decline in the average age of brands in Millward Brown's Top 100 Global Brands survey, moving from eighty-four years old in 2006 down to sixty-four in 2012.[7]

Uber, an on-demand car service with the tagline "Everyone's Private Driver," is a case in point. Users can request a private car via a smartphone app and use their phone to monitor their designated vehicle's arrival, knowing exactly when it will arrive. Their ride is charged to a credit card on file, and users can rate the service after their ride, ensuring that drivers will maintain their cars and offer great service. Drivers receiving ratings below 4.6 are fired. Uber has smartly tied in with businesses such as Nordstrom to propel word of mouth and enhance their image.

Uber was founded in 2009 and within three years had expanded to twenty-five countries and had received nearly 200,000 Facebook "likes." Uber and services like it, such as Lyft and SideCar, were just the threat that traditional taxi cabs needed to embrace innovation. Enter Flywheel, a start-up that partnered *with* taxi cabs to offer nearly the same services. Consumers were craving innovation in private transportation—most notably accountability by drivers and the ability to know when a cab would arrive. As Clayton Christensen points out in his book *The Innovator's Dilemma*, established companies often miss out on innovation opportunities.[8] And most innovation is not happening in established brands.

Heritage as Baggage?

In my research, I've found that we're not only more trusting of new things but also increasingly wary of brands and products that *don't* innovate. Products that have "stood the test of time" are OK for a retro thrill, but aren't as enchanting as the wizardry made possible by today's technology. For the first time, heritage can be baggage. Reverence for legacy brands, with a few notable exceptions, has diminished. Why? It has to do with an uptick in consumers' sense of individuality and self-reliance—a phenomenon we'll explore in more depth in the next chapter. Today's consumers are less interested in aspirational brands; rather than admiring brands, they're more interested in brands that admire them, know them, and serve them.

Heritage brands have great opportunity as long as they continuously innovate. Benjamin, a luxury traveler, says,

> I've paid very hefty prices for rooms in grand old hotels that turned out to have terrible Wi-Fi. It's impossible to feel like I'm in a luxury hotel when the Wi-Fi reminds me of using a dial-up connection in my mom's kitchen. That's unacceptable. How can they not be keeping up with what travelers need? I stayed at the Four Seasons in Toronto, and they had thought of everything. I was completely connected, and the hotel was tricked out with loads of new technology. A hotel can be elegant and rich with tradition and still know what today's travelers need.

As John Digles, executive vice president and general manager of MWW, points out, "The biggest risk with being cool is that someday you won't be. You have to constantly reinvent yourself."[9]

Even products that are difficult to advance technologically (like soup and shoes) can still showcase the spirit of innovation through technological displays, apps, and social media. For example, Adidas' wall of virtual footwear features their entire collection of shoes in virtual 3-D format. Prototypes are available that consumers can try on for size, and after ordering, the shoe is shipped directly to their home. Adidas shoes appear more advanced because of the futuristic way they're displayed, and sales have increased between 77 to 500 percent in the stores that feature the virtual wall.[10] Similarly, retailers ranging from Brooks Brothers to Victoria's Secret have 3-D body scanners that electronically detect a shopper's size and shape and recommend particular brands and styles to match the user's figure. These kinds of innovation put the juice back into shopping, and intelligent use of technology shows harder-than-ever-to-impress consumers that companies are listening, thinking, and actively trying new things to satisfy them.

Beloved "mature" brands such as Mattel's Barbie stay relevant to a new generation of users by incorporating technological features. Barbie's Digital Makeover Mirror has plenty of hot pink plastic and girly girl features, but also incorporates an iPad and facial tracking technology—just enough magic to satisfy today's stimulation-demanding kids. An upscale Atlanta steakhouse hasn't changed its menu in twenty years, but saw a 30 percent uptick in wine sales after it put its extensive wine list on iPads. The interactivity, notes, and reviews have been a hit with their customers and elevated the perception of an ancient establishment.

• • •

Consumers are hungry for "new." New products and new experiences. Innovation is a demonstration of the coolness, smarts, and consumer-centricity that today's shoppers demand. Innovation that's tied to technology gets even higher marks. It's no wonder that the Neuro Sleep that Sara has come to rely on has a name that speaks innovation with a techno edge.

Marketers who understand our thirst for what's new and our trust in innovation know that they need to delight and inspire shoppers with a dose of technology—something we'll discuss more in Chapter Four.

Consumer Empowerment

According to Edelman's highly regarded "Trust Barometer," the source trusted by the largest majority is "people like me."[11] Before the Internet, "people like me" would have been friends and acquaintances at work, school, or over the backyard fence. Social media have given "people like me" a huge megaphone and made them among the most powerful marketers in the world.

"I trust what Amy recommends," says Emma, a thirty-year-old photographer. "She has a blog, Cooking with Amy, that I read, and I follow her on Facebook. She gave a thumbs-up to a fatless deep fryer I would never had tried without her recommendation. I love it." Maggie, a fifty-four-year-old avid golfer, says that she was warned away from a discount golf store by online reviews from other golfers who told her their customer service was lacking.

Online luxury fashion retailer Net-a-Porter has a ticker-tape-type banner of the products other shoppers (called "the world's most stylish women" on the site) are buying or putting into their baskets. "It's kind of cool to see someone in Denmark or Taiwan or France shopping with you, to see what they're buying," said Liana. "It gives the site huge credibility too."

With trust for businesses at an all-time low, consumers increasingly rely on the words and actions of other shoppers to guide their purchases. Keller Fay Group, a word-of-mouth research and consulting firm, estimates that there are one trillion conversations going on about brands in the United States every year.[12]

Five-Star Commerce

Recommendations and reviews allow new products to move more swiftly into the hands of innovation-hungry consumers. And they are the assurance many need to trust and try new retailers and brands. Joan, a thirty-something online shopper, sums it up for many: "I don't trust websites that don't include product reviews. What are they trying to hide?"

Marketer-generated messages certainly have an impact on the perception and awareness that people have of brands and products, but they're far less trusted than the words of other consumers. More than 70 percent of consumers say they trust reviews, an increase of

15 percent in four years.[13] Eighty percent of consumers said that they changed their mind about buying a product after reading a negative review they found online.[14]

According to my own research, when it comes to trustworthiness, reviews written by other consumers are second only to the recommendations of friends and family. Except for electronics and cars, they are even more trusted than professional reviews.

In addition to the star count, the *number* of reviews sends a message to consumers about the popularity of a product or service. So, for example, two 5-star reviews are less trustworthy than one hundred 4.5-star reviews. In part this is because consumers are aware that there are plenty of fake reviewers out there. Clearly it's essential that brands and retailers encourage and facilitate reviews.

Consumers typically post reviews when they're either very happy or very unhappy. Slightly more consumers will post only positive reviews than those who are willing to post both positive and negative reviews. As Carmen said, "You know what they say, if you can't say anything nice, don't say anything at all. I only post a negative review if I'm really mad."

As it matures, the culture of online reviewing is evolving. Although consumers are increasingly comfortable leaving reviews, many are also tiring of what Elise describes as "working for free," and are leaving fewer reviews now than they did a year ago. Consumers tell me that the conditions for reviewing are especially dependent on how emotionally connected they feel to a retailer. "Nordstrom lets me send back anything without even paying postage, so I try to leave reviews when I have time to help them out," says Elise.

A robust review platform and the ability to filter reviews by demographics or geography are increasingly important to consumers—and therefore to the success of brands and retailers. And according to my research, there's lots of room for improvement in encouraging and facilitating product users to submit reviews. Beyond their emotional attachment to a retailer or feelings about a product, here's what consumers tell me motivates them to review: an email request with a tone of gratitude, being thanked for previous reviews, the ability to see when their review has been helpful to others through review rating functions, and the chance to win a prize or a gift certificate.

Facilitating customer commentary and reviews has another benefit for marketers. Positive comments create an illusory snowball effect. Our "herd instinct" kicks in, and what shoppers might have liked, they tend to like a lot more after reading positive comments. Negative reviews do not generate the same response. Consumers tend to be more skeptical of negative social influence.[15]

Power to the People

The consumer power of ratings, reviews, and social media has contributed mightily to the diffusion of innovation. It has also given voice to the average Joe and Jane and created a new consumer mentality of empowerment.

Once upon a time, there was a hierarchy that guarded the gates to fame and fortune. Top models, pop musicians, and television stars got there by pleasing the "experts" otherwise known as agents and executives. Today, *consumers* are the experts and are increasingly influential in helping promote brands, products, and celebrities.

Aspiring stars now have the ability to circumvent traditional routes and gatekeepers through the powerful voice of the consumers who are their champions. Justin Bieber and *Sports Illustrated*'s two-time cover model Kate Upton both rose to prominence through YouTube videos, and the best-selling novel *Wool* was initially self-published.

Bank of America, Netflix, and Verizon have experienced the harsher side of that consumer muscle—all have been forced to reverse new fee policies because of consumer outrage fueled by social media. Likewise, when a British Airways passenger didn't get an immediate response from the airline about allegedly lost baggage, he targeted all 302,000 of British Airway's Twitter followers and purchased promoted tweets to vent his anger.[16] Never before have consumers had so much power and such great ability to make or break products and businesses.

Review and ratings sites such as Yelp make or break local businesses. Karl detailed a horrifying example of plumbing gone wrong. "In all my years of homeownership, I've never had a problem like this. The plumber tried to do the electrical work, and he wasn't qualified. He crossed wires, and we ended up flooded with, well, waste under the house. To make matters worse, his company would not take responsibility. My wife posted a scathing review on Yelp, and within days he made amends. I think we would have ended up having to go to court without Yelp." On a happier note, Karl also said that one of his wife's Yelp reviews was responsible for a mom-and-pop picture framing shop's getting the success they deserved. "We'd been going to Westlake Art and Framing for twenty years, and they are better than fancy, high-priced framing shops. Bad location though. My wife posted a great review, and the next time she went to the shop, the owner said that they were packed with new business and that people were driving from twenty miles away to go to their shop!"

Consumers not only have the ability to learn about and trust products through their use of technology but also like having the power to champion the little guy. Investment through crowdsourcing platforms like Kickstarter has given everyone the opportunity to be an investor—and, more important, a champion. It takes consumer voice to a new level, and the emotional benefits are huge. Kickstarter has a 45 percent success rate for the full funding of campaigns.[17]

For example, Judith had been attending "purse parties" to snap up Sarah Oliver knitted handbags for years. The bags are made by a group of seniors (average age eighty-eight) in a retirement community who call themselves "The Purlettes + 1" (+1 is the lone male knitter in the group). When Sarah Oliver wanted to start a bridal collection, she turned to Kickstarter and quickly funded her nearly $30,000 goal. More important, she turned consumers into advocates and deepened their affection for the brand. "I am so excited," said Judith. Although Judith has never met Sarah Oliver or her Purlettes, her sense of involvement and belonging is evident in her comment, "We did it!" According to Sarah Oliver, "The Kickstarter campaign plus our use of Facebook, Twitter, LinkedIn, and Instagram contribute to an important emotional connection with our customers. This connection is what helps us stand out among our competitors."[18]

• • •

Once people have power—whether they exercise it through Yelp or Kickstarter, or by liking or linking on social media—there is no turning back. Consumers know their influence, and it has permanently affected their expectations and relationships with retailers and businesses.

Consumer empowerment has contributed to a less reverential relationship with brands and products, which means that marketers need to work harder to engage and involve consumers—something we'll discuss in Chapter Six.

Faster Ways of Thinking

Through our use of technology, we've become mental speed demons. Our sense of time, ability to focus, and capacity for attention have shifted gears. Because our malleable, adaptive brains respond to our experiences, the areas we use become even more efficient, faster, and more powerful, and what we don't use becomes less effective. In other words, our brains have adapted to a new, digital world, and we're neurologically different as a result.

That digital world is a place where we scan and view rather than read, and where we're bombarded by stimulation and constant interruptions. It is an environment that trains us to want everything faster and to crave stimulation. We're more easily distracted, and we have less tolerance for ambiguity—and nearly everything else that requires patience.

The shift in our neurology is driven not only by the loads of information we take in but also by the often accompanying anxiety to keep track of all that information and an expectation that we be available around the clock—which requires speed and often robs us of focus. In his book *iBrain: Surviving the Technological Alteration of the Modern Mind*, Gary Small describes the resulting mental state as "continuous partial attention."[19]

It takes an average of sixty-four seconds to recover your train of thought after an email interruption.[20]

Our lack of focus is a partial explanation for the popularity of products like Plated, a delivery service that provides every single ingredient down to little baggies of salt and pepper—to make "home-cooked" meals. Plated and the many services like it take the "cake mix" concept and put it on steroids. They address not only our craving for "fast and easy" but also the forgetfulness and anxiety that accompany a lack of focus. Even canning is making a comeback due to kits and automatic jelly makers that truly require only sugar and fruit—focus and patience are optional. Ball Mason jars are experiencing the highest sales ever in their 125-year history.

The consumers I've interviewed appreciate kits and semi-prepared products not just because they're easier and faster but also for peace of mind and anxiety reduction.

Lisa, a busy working mother, says, "I always seem to forget something, paprika or onions or something, and that means another trip to the store. Or I get there and round steak is on sale, but I can't remember if I have peppers, so I buy more and get home and there they were; now they might be wasted." Obviously it's not just convenience that consumers are looking for—it's also a way to accommodate their increasingly overloaded, less focused minds.

The sweet spot in semiprepared dinners is fifteen to thirty minutes of prep time. Any less and it "doesn't count."[21]

Time Warp: The Need for Speed

Those who digitally engage the most will experience this neurological shift more intensely. And because our brains are the most malleable when they're developing, children will experience these effects more powerfully and permanently. In focus groups that I conducted, older members of Generation Y, those in their late twenties and early thirties, were adamant that they were really very different from their younger cohorts. "My younger sister is constantly on her cellphone; she just can't stop," said Amy, twenty-nine, of her sister who is nine years younger. Pamela, thirty-three, describes a similar scene at her office: "They are constantly distracted; I walk by and they're sort of working but also texting and checking Facebook."

To demonstrate how our minds have adapted, consider a typical high school task: writing a research paper. Baby Boomers most likely went to their local library, scoured card catalogues, took longhand notes, and painstakingly typed their papers on a typewriter. Their challenge was in finding information. They memorized things like how to spell words, because reference materials weren't readily available and the process of checking was time consuming. And they were careful and precise when typing—correcting took time. Baby Boomer brains were trained to focus, pay attention to detail, be patient, and have fortitude. Haste meant waste.

Fast-forward to today. The Baby Boomer challenge of finding information is less relevant—information is extremely accessible. Memorization and precision are less essential as well—it's easy to check facts and spelling. This means that those brain activities don't get the workout today that they did for previous generations of high school students. Today's young brains are heavily focused on scanning and processing mountains of information. Their brains are trained for speed.

But it's not only the young who are increasingly addicted to speed. Their saturation in and early use of technology makes them ultra-primed to require more stimulation and become more easily bored—but everyone's brains are changing. We're all less patient and less able to focus, and we all want things faster. It's no wonder we've replaced the word "trend" with "trending." We barely alight on a new idea long enough for it to be a trend; it's just zipping by or "trend*ing*."

Ellie, thirty-seven, says she's bored with shopping in stores. "I used to love to browse. Now it feels boring. I think part of it is that I browse online almost every day. I can see everything, every size is there, what matches. It's so much faster. I hadn't realized how time consuming it was to go to stores, plus there isn't much to see—at least compared to online, when I can check four or five stores in a half hour." Most consumers still like to shop in stores—today. But unless retail evolves to incorporate more technology into the mix, Ellie's attitude will become the dominant one. Chapter Four is full of ideas about how to do this.

Stimulation Junkies

Here's a secret: multitasking isn't really multitasking. What we think is multitasking is actually our mind's quickly shifting back and forth between tasks—it can actually be a form of distraction for eager, stimulated, and easily bored minds. Our brains are not actually capable of focusing on two things at once. This explains why short interruptions, even of less than three seconds, doubled the number of errors on simple tasks in a recent study.[22]

- More than 68 percent of adults who own multiple devices use two or more screens simultaneously to "graze" unrelated content.[e]
- Nearly 40 percent of time spent on tablets is spent doing something else simultaneously.[f]
- Mobile media consumption tripled from 2009 to 2013.[g]

Stanford communications professor Clifford Nass studies how humans interact with machines. He notes that technology-enabled multitasking results in serious changes to the brain. "For adults it has effects on their cognitive and thinking skills. For younger kids we're seeing effects on their emotional development."[23]

Interruptions influence how we make purchase decisions. A UCLA study examined how participants made purchase decisions across a wide variety of categories—from high-priced luxuries to hiking trips. The authors found that brief distractions interrupted "detail-oriented and price conscious" decisions in favor of "goal-oriented, price insensitive" decisions.[24]

Minds that are bombarded with stimulation get bored more easily, and for many the solution is *more* stimulation. When we become habituated to high levels of stimulation, ordinary downtime and relaxation can feel empty and boring, so we gravitate toward more stimulation—which further habituates our senses. Ultimately, our ability to focus takes a hit when snippets do the trick.

Abundant choice and stimulation affect our decision making in another way: we make riskier decisions when we're overloaded with choices. A recent study found that people faced with larger numbers of options did less research per option and were more swayed by risky outliers.[25]

For marketers, knowing how consumers think differently is essential information:

- Consumers will spend less time exploring detailed information and will consider a wider variety of sources when searching for product solutions. New and novel ideas and products have a much greater opportunity for consideration than ever before—but the emotional connection has to be made quickly.
- Consumers will look for faster, simpler solutions to match the way they think. For example, brands that simplify consumer decision making are 115 percent more likely to be recommended.[26]
- It's simply going to take more intensity to get the attention of consumers and for them to feel inspired to pull the trigger on a purchase. What's required is not just ramped-up messaging but also more intense products, experiences, and promotions.
- Consumers will get bored more easily: with the products they own; with any impediment to purchasing, such as waiting in line; and with long explanations.
- Consumers will increasingly rely on faster, more symbolic forms of communication rather than the written word.

IWWIWWIWI

When we can get what we want when we want it—be it new shoes, medical information, research for a paper, or an update on a cousin's wedding—we come to expect immediate solutions. Impatience is the new virtue. Consumers respond to just-in-time information and ignore news before they need it. IWWIWWIWI (I want what I want when I want it) has never been more essential to satisfying the expectations of today's consumers.

Popcorn has been around for literally thousands of years. It's been served in theaters and at sporting events since the 1900s. Because it's inexpensive, it surged in popularity during the Great

Depression. Popcorn exploded in popularity during World War II, when sugar rations diminished candy production. In the 1950s, Coca-Cola and Morton Salt helped the Popcorn Institute convince consumers that popcorn was the perfect companion to their new television sets. The microwave reenergized sales of popcorn once again in the 1980s with ad claims like "You shouldn't have to wait for great-tasting popcorn." Today, the fastest growth in popcorn is in ready-to-eat packages, which grew nearly 12 percent last year (compared to a less than 1 percent increase in microwave popcorn). Colleen Bailey, brand director of Orville Redenbacher's, told *Advertising Age*, "Microwave popcorn at its inception was all about convenience, having only to wait three minutes to get warm delicious popcorn. But as times have changed, the definition of convenience has changed."[27] For many, three minutes has become simply too long to wait.

The breathless anticipation of the 3-D printer makes sense. Resource CEO Kelly Mooney describes it as the ultimate "maximum immediate gratification." Think it, want it, have it.[28]

Waiting? That's for yesterday's shopper. A one-second delay in the time it takes to load a web page typically results in a 7 percent reduction in purchases.[29] Waiting to check out feels like punishment to shoppers. Not that shoppers have ever liked waiting, but today it feels personal. Herb described a recent visit to a new "fast" food chain near his office: "Why couldn't they get another clerk up here? Didn't they see people were waiting? There were six people behind that counter and six people waiting in line. Why? It's so disrespectful. I'm not going back."

From on-the-floor checkout to paying with your smartphone to speedier online checkout, smart retailers are finding ways to satisfy speed-oriented shoppers. For example, luxury retailer Selfridges is now offering a drive-through pickup service for online orders. Removing impediments to purchase—most notably wait time—is essential.

Science writer Sam McNerney points out that a person's perception of wait time is more important that the actual time he or she spends waiting. Attacking the psychological issues behind the frustration with waiting, such as boredom and fairness, by offering consumers distractions or a well-orchestrated queuing process, has the same effect as decreasing the actual wait time.[30]

Naturally, Gen Y, who are digital natives, are the most sensitive to waiting, which is why they're the heaviest users of same-day delivery services, despite the costs. A Shop.org survey found that this generation of shoppers was more than twice as likely as average consumers to pay for same-day delivery services.[31]

IWWIWWIWI is behind three psychological hurdles to purchase. Here's what the hurry-up mentality means to marketers and retailers, and what they can do about it.

> *Anticipating needs squelches impatience.* Marketers can no longer wait for consumers to tell them what they need—they have to anticipate future needs. By the time someone can articulate what she wants, she's frustrated that she doesn't have it. Understanding your consumer's life and figuring out what she'll want next—whether it's a product alteration, a faster way to check out, or more excitement—before she even knows she wants it tames impatience and creates a bond.
>
> *Immediate solutions calm exasperation.* Consumers go from zero to exasperated in less time than ever. In the time it takes for a customer service agent to check with her manager, a customer's opinion can shift all the way from happy to hopeful to exasperated to angry. Preparing in advance or empowering sales and service personal to implement their own on-the-spot solutions provides the type of immediate response that consumers increasingly demand. You can also

avoid exasperation by streamlining and simplifying the processes by which consumers come to know, want, and buy
products.

Confidence quells anxiety. An unexpected side-effect of
IWWIWWIWI is the anxiety that accompanies wanting,
waiting, and wondering. Consumers who are more demanding
and emotional are reassured by calmness and confidence—
they can relax knowing that they're in capable hands.

Out with the Old

Consumers have clearly fallen in love with "new." But what to do
with the old?

In the dark recesses under Michelle's bathroom sink is a nearly
full bottle of shampoo that's at least five years old. She won't throw
it out because "that would be so wasteful." But she hates it. So
she tries to ignore it. In almost every home I've visited to conduct
ethnographic research, I've found at least one unwanted product
that was often several years old. It might be hiding under the sink
or stuffed in the back of a kitchen, dresser, or cabinet drawer or in
the bottom of a freezer or collecting dust in the garage. I've found
everything from disposable razors to diet soda, from frozen fish to
thong panties. Waste is a source of guilt to most Americans. We're
a country built on Puritan values. And though we've adjusted to
the idea of buying and having more, we still hold on to the notion
that wastefulness is a sin.

The speed with which consumers sample and embrace what's
new is matched only by how quickly they get bored with what they
perceive to be old. Technology and clothing are the biggest sources
of waste angst. "If I could give this to someone who would use it,
I would. I mean it's a perfectly good; I just prefer reading real
books," says Hank of his Kindle. The cognitive dissonance aroused
by the mixed emotions of desire for the new and shame about waste
is a problem for consumers.

How do consumers manage this conflict? In part through Goodwill stores, resale shops, buying or swapping parties, yard sales, and, like Janine from the introductory chapter of this book, selling on eBay. But there's an opportunity for the companies that find ways to give consumers an "out."

Through trade-ups, trade-ins, recycling or donation programs, repurposing, and even image management, consumers get the reassurance they need to purchase "new." For example, H&M will recycle unwanted clothing in exchange for discounts on new merchandise, and jewelry stores will often take back merchandise for trade-ups.

Taking it a step further, Patagonia's advertising campaign is a plea for consumers to buy less, and they also sell used clothing in several of their stores. Apparently just the association with a company that takes a stand against wastefulness is enough to tamp down the guilt of buying—annual sales at Patagonia have increased by almost 38 percent in the two years they have been running the campaign.[32]

As a professor, I'd like to think that the textbooks I assign never fall into the "unwanted" category. Unfortunately, that's not the case. Knowing that, bookstores are innovating. Paula Haerr is a popular trend forecaster in the college bookstore industry and VP of retail services for Connect2One. According to Haerr, "There is abundant competition for used textbooks in the online market. Campus stores are therefore finding unique ownership options to offset some of that competition, most notably rental options for textbooks. New, used, and even digital books can now be rented."[33]

Ownership issues and the need for new have also spawned the swift and exuberant adoption of a host of peer-to-peer (P2P) product-sharing services made possible by consumers' ability to connect via the Internet. People are renting out or sharing spare rooms, parking spaces, cars, and even dogs.

Symbol Power

"Pictures, pictures, pictures, he's always wanting me to send him pictures," said Susan of her boyfriend of three months. "Do you mean, like, sexting?" I asked. "No, I don't do that. He wants to see what I'm wearing to work, of me in a tank top, whatever."

As the adage goes, "a picture paints a thousand words." Today we've taken that idea and run with it. The super-speedy adoption of Instagram and Pinterest, the migration of Facebook postings from primarily words to primarily photos, and the ubiquity of photo text messages are testaments. Photos and videos are fast, easy, emotionally potent, and evocative—which makes them essential in an era when we have less patience for writing or calling yet are hungrier than ever for human connection.

In 2002, I conducted a study for a major cellphone manufacturer as they were preparing to launch the first camera phone. The purpose of my involvement was to determine how consumers would use photos, in order to inform the messaging of the launch. Initially the group I was studying sent posed or artistic photos similar to what they might have taken with a film camera—a remembrance. But the group quickly caught on that photos that were unusual, quirky, or provocative would elicit a greater response from others. Their photo content shifted away from what might be saved to remember an event or a person toward a more immediate expression and a way to connect emotionally. I saw how, even in its earliest stages, photo messages shifted home photography from a medium of stored memory to a vehicle for connection.

- In October 2012, Facebook users uploaded 300 million photos a day, up 20 percent from earlier in the year.
- Facebook posts that have photos generate 53 percent more "likes" and 103 percent more comments than text-only posts.[h]

Consumers increasingly skim and scan rather than read—favoring photos, visual cues, and symbolism over words. It's an ideal context for a social shopping website and app like Wanelo (want, need, love), which is a runaway success. Wanelo looks a lot like Pinterest. There are lots of lovely photos, masterfully designed and visually juicy sections, and the ability to see what your friends admire and to be admired for your own taste. But Wanelo differs from Pinterest in that you can click on any image and be taken to a site where the item is for sale. In two years Wanelo has acquired eight million users (primarily young women and girls) who spend an average of fifty minutes a day wanting, needing, loving—and buying—the products they see on the app or website. Five million products are saved for later consideration a total of eight million times a day.[34]

The Hidden Brain Power of Our Unconscious Minds

Although we'd never admit it, partly because we're unlikely to be aware of it, most of our purchase decisions are driven by unconscious cues. For example, car studies have found that consumers tend to purchase cars they emotionally relate to—ones that represent their lifestyle and personality. They then look for data to justify their decisions. Car specs are important, but not to inspire someone to purchase a particular car; it's vice versa: they're used to validate a car that's already been chosen.

Through all five senses, we're exposed to millions of bits of information and stimuli every second. Obviously we can't attend to all of it. We therefore focus consciously on what's new, threatening, and especially interesting, and on problems that need to be solved. The rest—which represents 99.99 percent of the information we receive—gets sent to "internal processing," formally known as our unconscious mind and colloquially known as things like gut reactions, cravings, habits, and impulses. The unconscious mind may be hidden from us, but that doesn't diminish its power. The fact that people generally—and mistakenly—believe that they make decisions logically and consciously only increases its influence. Let me give you an example.

Some time ago, I conducted a two-part study for a frequently purchased, low-involvement grocery store product. In the first part of the study, I had consumers "shop" a mock grocery shelf packed with variations of the package I was testing and competitor products. They could choose three or four products they'd like to "buy." Nearly everyone who chose the product I was testing picked a package that had a slightly off-kilter logo, part of which was cut off on the top of the package. I later brought those who had chosen the off-kilter logo into another room and gave them just two packages to consider: the one they chose and another that had a straight, fully visible logo. In nearly every instance, they thought they had chosen the straight logo and had plenty of good reasons for their decision: "I think it should be straight so that you can read it," "I think it's disrespectful to cut off the top of the logo," and so forth. What made sense to them when they were thinking about it wasn't in keeping with how they would have acted in a normal grocery store. Although the consumers weren't consciously aware of it, the off-kilter logo was what grabbed their attention in a crowded shelf space. Because this was the type of product and purchase decision that doesn't typically get a lot of conscious attention and is easily replaced by its competitors (and vice versa), getting noticed was paramount.

Our brains typically delegate the processing of nonverbal messages to the unconscious mind; this is why symbolic communication has always been an especially potent marketing communication tool. Symbolic marketing cues often circumvent the more analytical and rational parts of the brain and make a direct connection to our emotion and memory centers. Images, scents, sounds, and symbols are emotionally loaded, and we process them quickly.

The difference with today's consumer is that those hidden, unconscious cues are even more influential to the purchase decision process. Interruption-driven, overstimulated, distracted consumers have less ability to focus and less conscious brain space available to make decisions.

Want more proof? Here are a few of my favorite studies that show us just how much those tiny unconscious differences matter when it comes to establishing consumer choice. Many of these influences have long been known and used by marketers; the key difference now is that in our stimulus-drenched consumer environment, their power is much greater.

Seeing Red   Color and light have a powerful influence on our unconscious minds, a fact that savvy marketers use to their advantage. For example, in a comprehensive study of logo colors, red was highly correlated with excitement; white and pink were associated with sincerity; brown with competence and ruggedness; and black and purple with sophistication.[35] Participants in another study felt that hot chocolate tasted better in an orange or cream-colored cup than it did in a white or red cup. The study also found that drinks consumed from pink containers are perceived to be sweeter.[36]

Red appears to have a particular power. Merchandise displayed on red backgrounds gets higher bids than merchandise displayed on blue backgrounds.[37] Waitresses wearing red uniforms get 16 to 24 percent higher tips from men than waitresses wearing any other color.[38] When HubSpot conducted a test of two web pages, everything about the test pages was exactly the same except that in one, the "Get Started Now!" call-to-action button was red, and in the other, it was green. The red button outperformed the green button by 21 percent.[39]

Research participants in a room containing a lamp mimicking sunlight were willing to pay 38 percent more for green tea and 56 percent more for a newspaper subscription than participants questioned in a room without a sun lamp.

Word Power   Just as colors are symbols with potent emotional power, so too are words. Without pausing to understand meanings, we often jump right into associations. For example, how much would you pay for a bottle of Kit's Tasty Red Wine? Would you pay more for Appellation Bordeaux Contrôllée Mis en Bouteille a la Propriété? In blind taste tests of identical wines, consumers indicated a preference for the taste of a wine with a fancy name—and they were willing to pay $2 more per bottle.[40]

In a different blind taste test of wine (wine is evidently a favorite topic among consumer researchers), consumers said that a $5 wine with a $45 price tag tasted better than a $5 wine with a $5 price tag. They even thought that the $5 bottle with the $45 price tag tasted better than a $90 bottle of wine with a $10 price tag. In another pricing study, researchers found that prices that take longer to say are perceived to be higher than shorter sounding prices. Whether consumers see the price or say the price, prices with more syllables and commas seem higher to them.[41]

Attach the word "organic" to a cookie, and consumers say they'll pay 23 percent more than they would for an identical regular cookie. They also perceive the organic cookie to be lower in fat and calories than its twin "regular" cookie. Whether or not consumers will actually make that purchase is less clear: in a taste test of identical cookies bearing "organic" or "regular" labels, consumers said the regular cookie tasted better.[42]

Words are so powerful that they can change our self-image. Research participants who were primed with words associated with aging, including "bingo," "old," "Florida," "gray," and "wise" walked more slowly following the experiment than did non-stereotype-primed participants.[43]

Product Placement   Products located in the center of a horizontal display get longer looks and are more likely to be chosen than those on the left or right. In one study, products to the left of center were chosen only 24 percent of the time.[44] Why? Bruce D. Sanders, author of *Retailer's Edge*, notes that our eyes move to the right when the left hemisphere of the brain, where we do the math, gets active.

Therefore, when we think we've gotten a good deal, our happy left side of the brain dominates, and our eyes shift right. It's an explanation for why right-of-center products are more frequently purchased than left-of-center products.[45] This preference for right over left has nothing to do with conscious or rational decision making. When asked to rate four *identical* pair of stockings, the pair positioned to the far right was chosen four to one over the pair on the far left. Even when experimenters suggested that the position of the stockings might have influenced their selection, participants' responses ranged from confused to dismissive.[46]

Research participants asked to judge the effectiveness of everything from acne cream to fabric softeners consistently felt that products placed closer to images of the desired effect were more effective. As the study's authors state, "Merely changing the spatial proximity between the image of a product and its desired effect in an advertisement influences judgment of product effectiveness."[47]

The Nose Knows   Olfactory cues have a strong influence on our perceptions, behavior, and unconscious decision making too.

- In one study, when research participants were exposed to the mild scent of a citrus cleaning product, they were tidier than the control group when eating a crumbly biscuit—and they were unaware of the scent or their behavior.[48]
- In another experiment, slot machines in Las Vegas sprayed with a pleasant scent received 45 percent more play than those left unscented.[49]
- Diners spent 20 percent more money in a restaurant scented with lavender than they did when it was scented with lemon or when it was not scented. They also spent 15 percent more time in the restaurant.[50]
- Students exposed to the scent of peppermint scored 26 percent more hits during a video snowball game and were more engaged

with the game than those who played in an unscented area, suggesting that peppermint scent might also result in more attentive shopping too.[51]

• • •

Symbols and sensory input (especially imagery) deeply influence consumer decisions, and that means that now, more than ever, marketers need to understand semiotics—the study of nonlinguistic signs and symbols. Messaging with an emphasis on nonverbal cues is the mental shortcut today's consumers need in order to quickly and effortlessly understand product benefits. We'll go deeper in Chapter Five, and learn more about how to intensify your marketing efforts in Chapter Seven.

New Ways of Connecting

We're a society that is, in some senses, more connected than ever. We can easily develop relationships with fellow dog lovers and wine lovers, and even future lovers we've yet to meet in person; stay in touch with classmates and colleagues we no longer see in person; and share our opinions with strangers we'll never meet. It's a paradox of our age that although we have more "friends" than ever, we increasingly feel unheard, unseen, disconnected, or alone. At the very least, this calls in question the quality of all these connections. For marketers, it's a crucial piece of the consumer environment to understand and contend with.

Virtual Relationships

In the twenty years that I've been teaching graduate psychology, technology has been responsible for a tiny change in behavior that's had a big effect on the friendships and connections among my students. Where once I'd enter the classroom to find my students chatting or sharing notes, today there is significantly less interaction. Instead, they're almost always glued to their phones or computers. And it's not just in the classroom that people are opting for their smartphones and computers over interacting with real, live human beings. It's at parties and concerts, on dates, at the beach, during family dinners, and even during sex. Yes, that's right. Nearly 20 percent of smartphone-owning young adults and 9 percent of Baby Boomers will check a text that comes in while they're having sex.[52] (Which makes you wonder if they're doing it right. The sex, that is.) Nearly one-third of Internet users report spending less time with their families since being connected to the Internet. And when they *are* with them, they may be simultaneously multitasking on the phone.[53]

Although many of us use technology to orchestrate and facilitate existing relationships, plenty of us have also given over big chunks of face-to-face time to technology-infused time with others. Fully 39 percent of Americans spend more time socializing online than they do face-to-face with other people.[54]

Why does this matter? Because deep relationships and a sense of belonging are essential to our physical, emotional, and mental health. Psychologically, we respond differently when our communication is buffered by technology. For starters, the neurons associated with empathy don't activate in the same way. We don't get that calming, bonding flow of oxytocin. Our natural tendency to understand and empathize with others is diminished with each layer of separation—from face-to-face, to voice alone, to text and email. Further, even when we are connecting in person—be it with a close friend or a sales associate (because, yes, even those fleeting transactions bond us to each other and our communities)—the distraction of our cellphones can interfere with genuine connection.

People who have used online dating services tell me that a photo and online description can be enticing. The next step, email exchanges, can be downright exciting. After talking on the phone and texting, people can come close to feeling sure they've finally met their soul mate. And then within thirty seconds of meeting in person, that "soul mate" can be ruled out. Even if their appearance exactly matches their photos. Obviously something essential happens when we're face-to-face with other people.

Also, the very aspects of technologically enhanced communication that we love so much—speed, reach, and the ability to craft messages (rather than engage in spontaneous dialogue)—maintain a level of superficiality and invulnerability that inhibits the authenticity and intimacy that are the foundation of connection and belonging.

So technology has made communication more convenient and has certainly facilitated the development of relationships, but in itself it's also less bonding and nurturing. This affects our sense of belonging as we gradually replace in-person communication with online communication. As a result, our high-tech, low-touch society has left consumers looking for a sense of connection and belonging—something they increasingly find online, including through brands and retailers.

A Binky for Adults

Perhaps one of the most pervasive and important ways we use technology to connect while still keeping our distance is text messaging. These days, "I'm speechless" is taking on a whole new meaning. Data messaging revenues will eclipse voice messaging revenues by 2014.[55] Nearly half of those under thirty-five say that text communication is as meaningful as voice communication.[56]

People I've interviewed say that texting is more convenient and gives them time to consider responses; they appreciate the immediate gratification of sharing experiences, thoughts, or emotions as the occur; and they always feel connected to other people. Few mention what they might be missing while their focus is directed downward, but they're keenly aware of feeling ignored when the people around them are multitasking on their phones.

Robert, for example, visits San Francisco's popular Saturday farmer's market less frequently than he did in the past. "It's crowded. But now with everyone busy looking at their cellphones, you can barely get through. It's like everyone thinks they're the only one there. No manners, no sense of community." Even if you don't intend to converse with the people around you, playing bumper cars because nobody sees you is isolating, even alienating.

For many the cellphone has become an adult binky. Instead of shouldering through messy, real-time social situations, we very nearly suck on our cellphones for comfort. Cellphone messaging in social situations is modern navel gazing—not just because our heads are directed downward, but also because it's a form of self-absorption. At the very least, when we're absorbed by our phones, we're less focused on the people, scenes, or events of the moment. And it's increasingly prevalent, and expected, even though we find it alienating and rude when others engage in it.

> People aren't the only things we ignore when we're so phone focused. Now that more than 50 percent of Americans own smartphones, they're ignoring checkout-line magazine and gum displays while waiting to pay for their groceries. Impulse purchases at the checkout lines are in steep decline. In the second half of 2012, sales of single-copy magazines fell 8.2 percent over the previous year, and sales of gum declined 5.5 percent.[i]

David Carr describes his experience of texting's intrusion into social interaction in his article "Keep Your Thumbs Still When I'm Talking to You." He calls cellphones "digital wingmen" in his take on texting at the South by Southwest Interactive conference, which he describes as "the annual campfire of the digitally interested." Says Carr, "At the conference, I saw people who waited 90 minutes to get into a party with a very tough door, peering into their phones the whole while, only to breach the door finally and resume staring into the same screen and only occasionally glancing up."[57]

Pamela attends several charity dinners a year, and she's noticed a trend: people ignoring table companions to text and tweet to people who aren't there. She describes it this way: "It reminds me of a high school dance where you clung to your friend because it was so awkward to feel like you might be alone. People ignore other people to focus on somebody who isn't there just so they won't have to face stressful social situations."

Socializing stressful? Even the most articulate, extroverted, and gregarious among us experience a touch of anxiety or stress in social situations. At its most fundamental level, anxiety is simply the body's preparation for action—our senses are sharpened. Small levels of stress and anxiety are proven to enhance performance. Still, it's uncomfortable. Therefore, people often take smaller steps toward anxiety-provoking situations than they can handle. Which is why at any given moment, at a table full of strangers, many retreat to the safety of their cellphones (aka binky). Practice diminishes the level of stress we experience. We're not getting that practice if we consistently resort to the technological alternative.

As a result of this sense of disconnection, retailers and brands that feel authentic, that create a sense of community and belonging through their values, that inspire consumers to connect with each other, or that appear to see and honor their customers will hit the mark in a major way. We'll talk about how in Chapter Five.

2

Isolation and Individualism

Right up there with food, water, and shelter is our need for human connection. It's the foundation of happiness and the source of meaning and purpose in life—yet we've never been more alone.

Psychological studies point to everything from withering immune systems to madness or death as the fate of those bereft of human touch and nurturing. Our need to belong and connect is rooted in survival. After all, we *are* born naked and helpless. A caveman who wasn't part of a community didn't last long—and even if he did, his genes wouldn't. He couldn't possibly have fought off wild animals, enemies, and the elements; procured food; and still had time for wooing and procreation without belonging to a group. So anyone alive today is descended from someone who valued human connection.

Today we find ourselves in a unique position. Although we're genetically predisposed to connect, we can actually survive on our own. And that's what we're increasingly doing. We're disconnecting from the time-consuming messiness and anxiety-provoking unpredictability of interdependence. We are putting more emphasis on the self and paying less attention, and feeling less obligation, to others.

It's not so much that people want to avoid their neighbors, or care about the lives and opinions of their online friends more than those of the person who sits next to them at work, or enjoy venting their rage at strangers. Many of these behaviors are emotional reactions to a changing world, and they are as self-protective and defensive as they are potentially offensive to others. People are becoming more "all about me" for a reason—and it's not because they're defective. It's evidence of fissures between the fundamental human necessities of dependence and interaction—and the reality of a more superficial, disconnected life.

The rise of what I'm calling "radical individualism" is a big shift in our psychology. So naturally it has also created a big shift in how we shop and our reasons for buying. Most notable is an increased emphasis on the fundamental need to be seen, respected, and connected.

We've gone from mass markets to market segments to market niches to micro niches to markets of one.
—Kelly Mooney[1]

In this chapter, I'll describe why we're emotionally disconnecting from others, and how this shift has changed us as people. I'll describe a cluster of societal changes that have resulted in a more individualistic, "all about me" kind of interaction. Our use of technology has played a big role in both accelerating and enabling individualism, and you'll therefore find a few of the concepts from the previous chapter redefined in this one.

• • •

We're pulled toward radical individualism for reasons having to do with technology, emotional isolation, and an increased need for self-protection.

Technology-fueled communication is faster and relies more on superficial sound bites and quick visual cues than on deeper and more personal ways of knowing both people and information. There is a new emphasis on creating a "postable" moment rather than on living in the moment, and a pull toward perceiving other people as audience members. Technology also supports the democratization of "fame" and an increased interest in becoming "famous" in lieu of being deeply known in the context of real relationships.

A decreased sense of connection within communities; fewer shared cultural experiences, such as television programs or daily newspapers; a greater sense of anonymity through online communication; and a sense of invisibility due to decreased eye contact—all these contributors to emotional isolation can fuel a cycle of anger, alienation, and further disconnection.

We experience an increased need for self-protection due to a decreased trust in the social establishments we hoped were there to support us: religious institutions, schools, businesses, government.

Interdependency and individualism exist on a continuum. We're moving *toward* more extreme individualism, but that doesn't mean we're entirely alone. It's a trend and a shift, not an absolute. Nevertheless, it has deep psychological consequences—and it has a profound effect on what motivates consumers to value and purchase particular brands.

TECHNOLOGY

Did you think your big brain was all about outfoxing the enemy? Scientists have long attributed the success and survival of the human species to the abstract thought and planning made possible by our comparatively large brains. After all, it's not like we can outrun a tiger or win a fight with a bear without brains that can build tools.

Advances in neuroscience are now demonstrating that it's not just the outfoxing and computational parts of the brain that set us apart—it's our ability to form large, flexible, collaborative networks and deep, long-lasting relationships. Our relatively large prefrontal cortex combined with the ability to understand another person's state of mind are also essential to our survival and success as a species. Most important, deep human connection is our strongest motivator—to learn, grow, impress, strive, and succeed.

Technology connects us to each other—in snippets, and only in certain ways. On one hand, there's no question that technology facilitates existing relationships and nurtures new ones: from quick texts to Pinterest postings, we can check in, keep up, or deepen relationships. And social media is a magnificent tool for learning about new things. For example, Facebook has been shown to boost the confidence and acceptance rate of first-generation high school students applying for college by helping them understand what to expect.[2]

On the other hand, what we share through technology is generally superficial. Digitally facilitated communication can be meaningful, but it's less intimate and spontaneous. And it often presents a facade of a real life. Technologically aided communication puts the emphasis on sharing information—at the expense of sharing time and life. Simply put, online connection is just not as meaningful as real-world connection. For example, a study comparing the emotional impact of online and in-person friendships showed that increasing the number of Facebook friends had no effect on subjective well-being, but increasing the number of real-world friends from ten to twenty had the emotional impact of a 50 percent raise in salary.[3]

More than 21 percent of Millennials agree that someone can be in a relationship without meeting in person. And 19 percent say that an online relationship is just as meaningful as an in-person relationship.[a]

Digital communication has also taken a big bite out of the time available to spend with other people face-to-face. And here's a new wrinkle: for many, online communication is preferred to in-person interactions because it's faster, easier, and tidier. It's yet another quick fix and one that can develop into socializing inertia.

Jules is one of several people I've interviewed in the past year to make this point. "I think sometimes people would rather just stay at home and peruse Facebook than meet a friend for a drink. It's impossible to be bored these days. There's so much more to do at home online by yourself, so it can make the urge to go out not as strong. I'm content at home watching videos, emailing, shopping online."

> Nearly 60 percent of social network users say they feel more connected to people now than they did previously. In the same survey, 55 percent of respondents also said they have less face-to-face contact with friends, and 32 percent said they feel lonelier now than they did previously.[b]

Becky echoes Jules's comments: "Back in the day, if you made a commitment, you had to go. People are more unreliable because they can text and say they're not going to make it. They have a way to get out of things. Plus it's just so hard to get people to commit to anything. It's more effort to get out, and people are so reachable in every other way. There are so many more distractions that keep people in instead of pull them out."

Though not the majority, a significant number of people whom I've interviewed have told me that long-range planning is nearly impossible because people don't want to commit, adherence to the commitments they do have is waning, and the easier and more stimulating (at least mentally) connections they make via their smartphones are often a fail-safe preference anyway. That also explains the sea of heads-down people you see at parks, bars, and ball games. They're with other people—but not really.

Surface Appeal

Carl Jung, the psychiatrist and scholar who taught us the value of seeing and accepting ourselves and others—warts and all—would likely have a few words to say about our use of digital communication. Everyone uses a persona to put his or her best foot forward and to smooth social interactions. Jung described it as "a kind of mask, designed on the one hand to make a definite impression upon others, and on the other to conceal the true nature of the individual."[4]

To smooth casual interactions and work collaboratively, we are very good at sharing the aspects of ourselves that we know will be accepted and admired, while hiding—sometimes even from ourselves—the uglier, less polished parts of our personalities. The problem is that when it comes to deeper relationships, if we only share superficially—only present that social mask—we never feel truly loved. How could we? We're receiving appreciation and feedback on only a fraction of our true self. Although we may appreciate approval of our facade, real emotional nourishment comes from sharing our full selves.

In her book *Alone Together: Why We Expect More from Technology and Less from Each Other*, M.I.T. professor Sherry Turkle wonders if "virtual intimacy" degrades our experiences of each other. She offers ample evidence of superficiality in our communication and experiences of each other because of our use of technology: "In the silence of connection, people are comforted by being in touch with a lot of people—carefully kept at bay," Turkle notes.[5] "We can't get enough of one another if we can use technology to keep one another at distances we can control: not too close, not too far, just right." And the editing, deleting, and retouching capabilities of online communication "let us present the self we want to be."

Turkle goes on to describe what's lost when we substitute conversations with emails or text messages, what she calls "sips" of connection: "Connecting in sips may work for gathering discrete bits of information or for saying, 'I am thinking about you.' Or even for saying, 'I love you.' But connecting in sips doesn't work as well when it comes to understanding and knowing one another." Turkle points out that we care for and tend to each other in face-to-face conversations by noticing tone and nuance and seeing someone else's point of view. That nuance and give-and-take are lost in online communications.

Superficiality reigns in another way. With shorter attention spans, mounds of data to digest, and an emphasis on speed, appearances are more important than ever. It's no wonder the beauty business is booming.

- In the past fifteen years, there has been a 542 percent increase in breast lifts, a 360 percent increase in tummy tucks, and a 103 percent increase in male breast reductions.[c]
- Nearly five million injection procedures (such as Botox) were performed in 2012.[d]
- Sales of prestige beauty products sold in department stores grew 18 percent from 2011 to 2013.[e]
- In 2005, the average age a girl started using beauty products was 17; today it's 13.7.[f]
- More than 42 percent of Millennial women follow beauty products brands on social media.[g]

Our emphasis on appearances makes the success of apps like Tinder a tiny bit more comprehensible. Tinder is a "dating" app—or, more correctly, a rating app. After entering your location, gender, and gender preference, you swipe through photos of potential matches giving each a thumbs-up or thumbs-down depending on his or her appearance. If two people match up (and thirty-five million had in the first eight months), they can begin the texting phase of their "romance." Within a year of launch, Tinder users had rated each other more than thirteen billion times.[6]

Superficiality isn't just for the youngsters. At a recent women's outstanding achievement awards ceremony, Christine noticed that the room was buzzing over the appearance of Heidi Klum. "Here we were, women who ran corporations, women who cured diseases, women who ran countries, for god's sake—and we're excited about a model? It's sad. And by the way, I include myself in that group that was excited."

Hello? Hello?

Today, everyone gets their say, but they're not always heard. Obviously we're not reading the feeds of hundreds of Facebook friends, thousands of tweets, or every blog and author we follow. You know it and I know it. We all know it and therefore often have a creeping sense that for all that "talking," we're not really being heard. Despite that, we receive just enough stimulation from these beeps, buzzes, and bits of information and feedback to keep us engaged and wanting more. It's similar to snacking on junk food all day. You're never really hungry, but you're never really nourished or satisfied either.

As Brené Brown, author of *Daring Greatly*, points out, "We're hardwired for connection. There's no arguing with the bioscience. But we can want it so badly we're trying to hot-wire it."[7]

Facebook users share 2.5 billion pieces of content on the site each day. YouTube users upload the equivalent of twelve years of video to the site each day.[h]

Even when we *are* heard, the superficial level of social media, which is really more like broadcasting, prevents the sort of conversation that is nourishing. Eileen, a thirty-year-old graduate student, described an experience that exemplifies the point: "I have a very casual friend that was apparently dumped by her boyfriend. I follow her on Facebook and started noticing kind of morbid sorts of quotes about heartbreak and then they got really gross, like she was bottoming out. I kept thinking I should say something, but Facebook didn't feel like the place, and really, I don't know her very well."

Eileen's friend was unusually forthright. Facebook *isn't* the place for depth and complicated emotions. Facebook is more commonly a platform for positive expressions—jokes, events, accomplishments, happy photos, and such. Dr. SunWolf, a professor of communication at Santa Clara University, where she developed the course The Science of Happiness, describes it this way:

> People continually wonder how happy they are compared to others, since we are creatures of social comparison. On Facebook, people show how happy they are by posting their happy activities. Facebook, however, causes us to wonder if we're less happy than our friends, since rarely does anyone post the downside of their lives—leaving us to assume that other people are more happy than we are. Studies show that the happiest people tend to engage in downward social comparisons (comparing their lives to those who have less), while unhappy people engage in upward comparisons (comparing their lives to those who have more). Even when we get the things we really wanted, we start to want more, due to hedonic adaptation (becoming used to the delights in our lives). This drives us to run on what is called the hedonic treadmill. Getting what we want never satisfies. We want still more happiness.[8]

Or as Jason Dubroy, VP managing director of shopper marketing for DDB Canada, points out, "Can anyone ever really be satisfied today? Once the buck stopped with your neighbor's lawn; now our baseline of comparison is the world."[9]

- German researchers have found that more than one-third of Facebook users have negative feelings after engaging with Facebook, usually envy.[i]
- A University of Michigan study found that the more people used Facebook, the greater their decline in life satisfaction levels.[j]
- A study of five hundred university students revealed that high frequency cell phone users tend to have lower grade point averages and higher levels of anxiety relative to their peers who used their cell phones less frequently.[k]

The Fame Game

Jessica's invitation to her high school prom received over one hundred Facebook "likes." Her date had spelled out "PROM?" with hundreds of votive candles and ringed the candles with dozens of long-stemmed roses. It was a visual feast, which was the point. The invitation was almost secondary. When I asked Jessica about the extravaganza, she said that everyone posted their "promposals" on Facebook, and the bar is high. Although the creativity is admirable, when it comes to promposals, it seems that the heartfelt intimacy of a prom invitation has been replaced by a quest for the admiration of the masses—otherwise known as fame.

Four times as many middle school girls would rather grow up to be the assistant to a famous movie star than the CEO of a major corporation or a Navy Seal. Three times as many would choose the assistant position over being a U.S. senator and twice as many over being president of Harvard.[10]

When preteens were asked what they wanted in their future, their number-one choice was "fame."[11] It's no wonder. From 1967 to 2007, fame had risen to become the most prominent social value communicated in top television programs targeted to tweens. In previous decades, fame was fifteenth out of sixteen values.

Meanwhile, "community feeling" sunk from first or second place in previous decades to eleventh place in 2007.[12] When asked about their generation (not just themselves), both generations of adults under forty ranked "to get rich" as the most important life goal of their generation, followed by "to be famous."[13]

So what does the Internet have to do with an increased interest in fame? It's related to those deep caveman instincts mentioned earlier: connection equals survival. The difference is that our "tribes" are much bigger and more far-flung these days. It starts with our basic human need to be seen and belong—which is heightened because of our increasing sense of invisibility. The reach of technology has widened our communities so that for many, "being seen" is akin to being famous.

It makes sense that the younger members of our community are the most captivated by the quest for fame. Through technology, they've always had the potential to connect well beyond their physical communities. And they've had more abundant opportunities for fame—or at least notoriety. In addition, they've grown up with the self-esteem movement, which we'll explore in the next chapter.

Yalda T. Uhls is a researcher at UCLA's Children's Digital Media Center and coauthor of some of the fame research mentioned earlier. "The hunt for fame, when tied to a skill, is not necessarily negative," Uhls says. "Many people want to be recognized for their work or talent. But when the desire is for fame for its own sake or for bad behavior, as in so many reality television shows, it can become destructive." Uhls points out that children typically don't understand the talent and sacrifices associated with achieving fame, and this can cause problems. "If they believe that fame is achievable without any talent or hard work, and then don't achieve fame, depression, negative self-esteem, anxiety, and more can result."

When asked about the role of social media in the quest for fame, Uhls sees a clear relationship between valuing fame and the use of social media. She says, "Children who use social media to frequently post photos and update their status value fame more than the children who do this less. I suspect that an excessive focus on social media, as well as the ability to take 'selfies' nonstop and post them, may be influencing people to think they should go after their fifteen minutes [of fame]. Children today are growing up in a world where they are aware that they can have an audience long before previous generations even understood the meaning of fame."[14]

> The promise of fame is what makes crowdsourcing and star contests so alluring and successful, particularly for the under-forty crowd. More than 120,000 people submitted photos of themselves performing specific actions, such as jumping, in the hopes of being chosen for a fraction of a second of fame in Pepsi's 2013 Super Bowl halftime advertisement.[1] And thousands participate in American Eagle's Project Live Your Life and Forever 21's Photo Booth contests, both of which are platforms for being "seen" by the masses, in venues that include a giant digital screen in Times Square.

The idea that you're a somebody if you are famous and a nobody if you're not feels like a death threat to the primitive, limbic "caveman" portions of our brains. This helps explain why so many are drawn to playing the numbers game with friendship and how they end up associating fame with security and a genuine connection. It's a cycle of self-involvement that ironically inhibits the very sense of belonging that's behind it all: broadcasting positive self-images results in bits of connection that are just nourishing enough to fuel more broadcasts, which take time away from conversation with others and put the emphasis on the self—the retouched and edited self, that is.

Living in the Moment vs. Posting the Moment

Raquel had the privilege of attending the 2013 White House Correspondent's Dinner. This is how she described the event: "There are three things I'll never forget: first of all the gowns—oh my god, gorgeous; second, President Obama is a great comedian; lastly, I was shocked to see people at my table texting or tweeting or whatever while he was giving his speech! Are you kidding me?" Were these texters, tweeters, and recorders in fact missing important emotional moments while trying to share them?

Social media has spawned another trend: recording (and even creating) events for the sake of what public relations and social media expert Greg Berardi calls "the postable moment."[15]

Nancy recently attended what she describes as "an amazing performance" of the San Francisco ballet. "There were all these cellphones in the air, people recording the performance. It was disruptive to me, and really they were focused on their phones instead of the performance, and I just can't believe they could feel it the same way than if they were just there and watching."

Cellphone videos are so ubiquitous at concerts that the Yeah Yeah Yeahs recently posted a sign at the entrance of their performance that read, "Please do not watch the show through a screen or your smart device/camera. Put that shit away as a courtesy to the person behind you and to [band members] Nick, Karen and Brian."

Paying attention to what's happening in the moment, otherwise known as mindfulness, is a hot topic in psychology these days, in part because of the new and noteworthy ramifications of our increasing lack of focus. In effect, we're pausing experiences to consider how they'll appear to others. Because our brains really aren't cut out to be fully—and especially emotionally—present with two experiences at once, we're shortchanging the psychological processing of experiences when we're focused on how they'll appear to others—in other words, living in our heads instead of living life. Which explains why so many people have described to me how they're happy *with* their lives but not necessarily happy *in* their lives.

For example, Evan, a college student I interviewed, showed me a video of his bungee jump. In the video, his expression was stoic, and he calmly said, "This is sick, man," as he flew backward in a holster over a massive rocky cliff. It seemed unnatural. As if he were performing. Indeed, he said that the bungee jump included a video ready for immediate posting on Facebook. Evan did receive lots of "likes" and comments from his friends. And perhaps that was a fair trade for his performance, maybe even more thrilling than what he might have experienced in the moment. But without a doubt, he did not experience the moment the same way he would have had he been less focused on how he appeared.

Psychologists aren't the only people concerned about how phones are affecting our social connections. In a two-minute viral video "I Forgot My Phone," viewers follow a young woman throughout a day of social activities where she is surrounded by people but basically alone—phones have taken precedence over human connection. The video received more than twenty million YouTube views within its first two weeks of posting; clearly this is a shift that many are struggling to understand.

Superficiality, performing instead of living, a sense of disconnection and invisibility—all of these technology-related shifts encourage self-focus, or what I'm calling radical individualism. At the same time, there's nothing more fundamental than the need to connect and belong. Marketers who are aware of this shift and the desire consumers have to feel relevant, seen, and connected can generate loyalty. Examples include responding immediately to Twitter complaints, offering ways to connect through Facebook contests, and showcasing humanity through jargon-free communication.

EMOTIONAL ISOLATION

We've always been a country that prizes individual contributions. From the Lone Ranger to Steve Jobs to movie stars—the individual who's the catalyst, leader, genius, or simply the face of triumph is who moves us. Never has that been more true than today. Our ramped-up quest to be "the one" has been catalyzed by the democratization of fame. From overnight Internet millionaires to reality television stars, social media sensations, and hotly followed YouTube sensations—anyone can be a star. Humility is increasingly taking a backseat to a focus on the attention that people crave more than ever as a way to be seen and to belong.

Although the average American isn't avidly pursuing stardom, there is an encompassing societal shift toward a self-focused life and away from an emphasis on the "greater good." *New York Times* columnist David Brooks recently described the findings of studies that analyzed the words used in Google's database of 5.2 million books published between 1500 and 2008. He notes a sharp increase in words and phrases associated with individualism, such as "self," "I come first," "personalized," and "standout," and a decrease in communal words and phrases such as "community," "collective," "share," and "common good." At the same time, words associated with moral virtue, such as "modesty," "compassion," "kindness," "honesty," "helpfulness," and "dependability" were on the decline. Brooks summarizes by saying, "Over the past half-century, society has become more individualistic. As it has become more individualistic, it has also become less morally aware, because social and moral fabrics are inextricably linked."[16]

Trust and Self-Reliance

In 1950, fewer than 10 percent of Americans lived alone. Today, it's over 28 percent.[17] Although living alone doesn't necessarily translate to being isolated or lonely, this shift speaks to the growth of independence in relation to interdependence. That said, there's also an increase in loneliness. The AARP conducts studies of loneliness, and in 2000, 20 percent of adults forty-five and older reported feeling chronically lonely. Ten years later, that number had jumped to 35 percent.

Multiple studies show an irrefutable connection between high levels of social trust and social support, and happiness. Social support and trust are also linked to more resiliency during crisis. In the United States, all three—trust, support, and happiness—are in decline.[18]

Dr. Jim Taylor is a business psychologist, an author, and a popular blogger for the *Huffington Post* and *Psychology Today*. He cites clear evidence that people are becoming more self-focused, self-referenced, and self-interested. He attributes some of this to the fact that people just don't know and interact with those around them as they have in the past. According to Taylor, "If we don't know others around us, we focus on ourselves. When people interact with others, empathy goes up and narcissism goes down."[19]

> Loneliness affects our product choices. Nonlonely people prefer products that are endorsed by the majority (80 percent) of previous customers. Lonely people prefer products that are not endorsed by the majority (ones that are preferred by only 20 percent of previous customers).[m]

There are a host of reasons behind our increased isolation, many of them mentioned earlier in this chapter. What's stunning is the multiplier effect. The less we interact, the more self-focused we become, and the less we interact. Robert Putnam, author of *Bowling Alone*, notes that there have been significant decreases in many of the fundamental and traditional activities that bond people to each other: meeting friends, socializing with family, knowing your neighbors. He found that social activities such as belonging to clubs increases happiness as much as doubling your income.[20]

Americans also have fewer close friends. In 1985, the mean number of close confidants was nearly 3; by 2004, that number had dropped to 2.08. The same survey found that the number of people who say that have no one with whom to talk through important matters had doubled to nearly 25 percent.[21] A 2010 follow-up to the study by one of its authors found that the number of confidants had dropped further, to 2.03.[22]

> In an experiment conducted in 2013, people who felt isolated or excluded made riskier financial decisions and had a greater appetite for gambling.[n]

Community Through Commonalities

My grandfather delivered coal in upstate New York during the winter and sold vegetables from the front yard of his house during the summer. My uncle, who was severely developmentally delayed, worked beside my grandfather. This was well before the days of political correctness, yet everyone who came to the house to buy vegetables knew and honored my uncle. He was part of the community and accepted for who he was—an example of how familiarity and contact create connection and belonging despite differences.

It's through interaction that we develop trust. It doesn't even have to involve a conversation—just unison does the trick. For example, in a Stanford study, research participants who were instructed to stroll around a campus in step with other people reported significantly greater trust in their fellow walkers than a control group of people who didn't walk in step.[23] As further proof of the psychological power of unison, donations for endangered butterflies were nearly 79 percent higher if the butterflies were depicted flying in rows and beating their wings in unison rather than simply fluttering about.[24]

Today, we often don't see eye to eye—literally. With myriad opportunities to fulfill our needs online, and our ever-present smartphones to distract and comfort us, we have less eye contact with people in our communities than ever before. And when we do interact, there's less in common to discuss. On any given morning, it's highly unlikely that most of your coworkers have watched the same television show, read the same newspaper, visited the same store, or eaten a similar meal. It's wonderful to have so many choices, to watch specific entertainment programming exactly when you want to, and to drill down deeply into the news that's of most interest. But at the same time, with fewer common community experiences, there's more emotional isolation.

Brands can serve as an emotional conduit to connection. The values and meaning of potent brands draw like-minded people together—at least in spirit. After analyzing multiple ratings and reviews of high-end stereo equipment, Jeff, a sixty-year-old executive from San Francisco, settled on a McIntosh system. He spent about 20 percent more than he'd planned. The system he chose got great reviews, but then so did almost every other system in his five-figure price range. Jeff made this decision, and the decision to spend beyond his initial budget, because of a tidbit of information he uncovered in his research: the Grateful Dead had used McIntosh amplifiers when they began playing together. Shoppers have always been attracted to brands that appear to be endorsed by trusted celebrities. But Jeff's decision to purchase a McIntosh had more to do with his craving for emotional connection than paying homage to his favorite band.

RUDE!

Rachel was happy to spend twenty thousand miles for an upgrade to business class on a flight from Boston to San Francisco. But even though she was used to the increasingly dehumanizing aspects of air travel, she wasn't prepared for the hostility and rudeness she encountered from her fellow business-class travelers that day. "A few people had multiple bags, and they'd completely filled the overhead bins before I arrived. I tried to move one in order to make room for mine, and this guy jumps up from his seat and yells at me for touching his bag. It was scary; he was so hostile. Everybody just sat there, nobody willing to move a bag, nobody willing to stand up for me."

With societal anxiety on the rise, with less in common and less time to engage in empathy-generating face-to-face communication, it's no wonder that rudeness also is on the rise. Rasmussen Reports found in 2012 that 76 percent of Americans believe that society is becoming ruder and less civilized.[25]

Rudeness is isolating and dehumanizing. Seventy-three-year-old Margaret says, "I go to the grocery store and people just leave their carts right in the middle of the aisle like they are the only people shopping. They talk loudly, their kids run wild. When I check out, the cashier never even looks up. What am I, just invisible?"

Margaret is not alone in her feelings and observations. Here are a few of the many comments I've collected in just the past year:

> I hate shopping in stores these days. Salespeople so often treat you like they're doing you a favor ringing up your purchase. They shove the change, purchase, and receipt at you all in one pile, wait for you to thank *them*, and then look annoyed if you take too long trying to get the change in your purse with one hand.

> What happened to civil discourse? All I see from politicians these days is rudeness, insults, they interrupt each other.

> I've stopped blogging. There are always comments that aren't constructive; they're just meant to offend. I had one guy that every single time would just write "delete." I'm putting my expertise out there for free, and you don't have to agree with me, but why not be civil?

> I think twice about using my directionals when I'm driving. Once it was a signal to others to make room and prepare; today it's just alerting the enemy. It's everyone for themselves out there now.

Rudeness hits us at a deeply emotional level. Minor affronts typically elicit a tinge of anger or disgust. More marked events, such as Rachel's experience with an abrasive fellow passenger, can produce heart-thumping autonomic nervous system arousal that is, in effect, our body's preparation for a fight. Why? Because rudeness communicates disrespect, invisibility, or irrelevance, which call into question our "pack status" and therefore our security.

I recently heard a speaker at a marketing conference brag about how he didn't win a particular account because he wore jeans and a T-shirt to the pitch. He sneered at the foolishness of the company he was pitching for letting something like his wardrobe get in the way of their seeing his genius. In fact, the speaker's arrogance prevented him from seeing what the rudeness of his dress communicated to the company. He was, in effect, telling the potential client that *his* values superseded *their* values and that he didn't intend to learn about or respect the hierarchy and ideals of the organization. Of course, that might well have been the truth—in which case, that speaker had a terrific fail-safe way of weeding out clients he wouldn't have enjoyed working with.

Rudeness shows a disregard for social norms, so it makes sense that our more individualistic society will have more rudeness. Obviously, those who are "all about me" won't care as much as about what's best for "all of us."

The aggravating problem is that rudeness is self-perpetuating. Because it feels like an attack, it typically inspires defensiveness. Sometimes that comes in the form of withdrawal—which leads to more individualism, fueling more rudeness. Other times it results in defensive combat—otherwise known as sinking to the other's level, which will also elicit a response that perpetuates even more rudeness.

All this is exacerbated by one of the misguided messages of the self-esteem movement: that only the insecure are concerned about what other people think. On the contrary—it's in our DNA to care about the opinions of others and to be sensitive to rejection. Living by the mantra "I don't care what anybody else thinks; I'm doing my own thing" further impairs our already waning abilities to manage the natural anxieties of socializing. If we think we should be above the very human inclination to care about the perceptions of others, we'll feel doubly defeated by rudeness.

Rudeness tops the list of customer service complaints in 2012. It jumped ahead of 2007 top complaints, such as uninformed employees or understaffed stores.°

Rising rudeness has not been caused by technology, but technology is accelerating the trend. Obviously, the less connected that people feel toward each other, the easier it is to misbehave. Anonymity is a form of disconnection that permits transgressions. In a study of how anonymity influences behavior, researchers found that people donated one-third less to unseen players in an online game when they were wearing sunglasses (which creates a sense of anonymity) than when they were without sunglasses. They also found that dimmed lights and darkness increased dishonest and self-interested behavior. Apparently even the *illusion* of anonymity results in more selfish and unethical behavior.[26]

People are more generous, honest, and polite when they feel seen and respected. And as we discussed in the previous chapter, people experience a deeper connection with others when they're interacting face-to-face rather than communicating through technology.

The relative anonymity of driving in a car demonstrates the point. Nearly every driver at some point has succumbed to rudeness, swearing, honking, or aggression. Driving in traffic combines adrenaline and anonymity. And as we know, anonymity breeds rudeness. And everyone who has spent time online—emailing, using social media, or reading comments threads—knows what happens when we have the absolute anonymity of the Internet, or even the partial shield of technology-buffered communication.

> - In 1998, one-quarter of American workers said that were treated rudely at work at least once a week. That percentage rose to one-half of workers in 2011, according to research conducted by Christine Porath of Georgetown University.[p]
> - In a 2013 survey of 2,896 social media users, 78 percent reported an increase in incivility.[q]

Societal rudeness has made people more defensive and self-protective. It's self-perpetuating and has contributed to a more individualistic consumer who is eager for civility.

Protecting consumers from rudeness in order to create a more appealing shopping environment means conducting more customer service training—and it also means rethinking rules about the customer always being right. Sometimes sequestering, censoring, or ejecting unsavory customers in order to elevate the marketplace is the sort of parenting and protecting that's now required by retailers. Online too.

SELF-PROTECTION

The Great Recession had a profound effect on the psychology of Americans. Fallout extends well beyond the financial impact that everyone experienced. Americans lost more than money—they lost a sense of security. The swift onset of the recession registered as a dizzying blow, and it left consumers much more wary and guarded.

The recession fostered a culture of frugality. Conspicuous consumption was replaced by conscious consumption. Spending patterns shifted toward a greater awareness of how money was spent and where consumers felt that they got the most emotional bang for their scarcer, more valued dollars. For example, pleasure products such as nail polish and cheesecake got a boost during the recession, while not-so-fun shoe polish and lawn fertilizer took a hit.[27] Elizabeth, a thirty-one-year-old office manager, told me about a $95 bottle of perfume she had purchased that she considered to be a value: "I can use it every day and it will still last a year!"

Even those who were still willing and able to spend freely during the recession registered the inappropriateness of showcasing their good fortune. Snagging a great bargain became the new status symbol of spending. In the wake of the recession, consumers still think more carefully about what they need and how they choose to spend their money. They still voice the mantra of saving—although what they do isn't necessarily what they say. Mintel conducted a study comparing where people say they've reduced spending to actual sales in those markets. The researchers found a vast discrepancy. For example, if consumers were reducing spending to the level that they claimed, out-of-home alcoholic beverage sales should have been reduced by 47 percent, when in fact actual sales experienced a 6 percent increase. Similarly, consumers said they were spending on average 32 percent less on their homes and gardens, but actual spending had increased 3 percent.[28]

The emotional impact of the Great Recession is part of the American psyche. More uncertain and less trusting, Americans are more protective of their resources. But for many, more conscious consumption began before the recession. Some reacted to a sense that life was out of control with a move toward simplifying and organizing their material world. For others, spending more consciously was related to environmentalism.

The triple whammy of the recession, the simplicity movement, and environmentalism has changed American consumption rules forever. Most notably, Americans are thinking more about what they buy. Knee-jerk buying has been replaced by a more empowered and determined insistence on value and emotional satisfaction, and a greater awareness of new options. As Julie, a young mother I interviewed during the recession, said, "I can't believe I used to spend like that. What was I thinking? I wasn't, actually."

Matters of Trust

On any given day, an assortment of headlines feeds a gnawing sense that the agencies and entities that are supposed to serve us— churches, schools, businesses, and especially government—are untrustworthy. Take April 2, 2013, for example. These were the news headlines on my Google homepage that day:

- "Ex-Firefighter, Girlfriend Charged in Virginia Arsons." The couple was suspected of setting the majority of seventy fires in the previous five months.
- "Lawmakers Charged in Plot to Buy Spot on Mayoral Ballot." U.S. Attorney Preet Bharara said the case was but the latest evidence that corruption in New York was "pervasive."
- "Ex-Schools Chief in Atlanta Is Indicted in Testing Scandal." Thirty-five Atlanta educators fixed student test scores for the sake of their own bonuses.

A greater number of "breach of trust" stories are coming at us these days, not just through the evening news or the morning paper, but throughout the day, through Twitter feeds, blogs, Facebook postings and home pages. To compound the effect, news is reported in a more sensationalist fashion today and by bloggers who are untrained in journalistic integrity—and by a few partisan journalists who have forgotten the art of journalistic integrity.

Jon Lovett, once a presidential speechwriter and more recently a television writer, gave a commencement address at Pitzer College where he spoke to the growing trend toward superficiality and its companion—decreased trust. "One of the greatest threats we face is, simply put, bullshit. We are drowning in it. We are drowning in partisan rhetoric that is just true enough not to be a lie; in industry-sponsored research; in social media's imitation of human connection; in legalese and corporate double-speak. It infects every facet of public life, corrupting our discourse, wrecking our trust in major institutions, lowering our standards for the truth, making it harder to achieve anything."[29]

In a recent Gallup poll, only 7 percent of Americans responded that they felt they could "trust government in Washington to do what is right just about always," and 14 percent felt that they could trust "most of the time."[30] Only 21 percent of Americans are satisfied with the "way things are going" in the United States.[31] Fewer than a quarter of Americans said they had "a great deal" or "quite a lot" of confidence in Congress, HMOs, big business, banks, organized labor, and television news. And fewer than half of Americans expressed "a great deal" or "quite a lot" of confidence in newspapers, the criminal justice system, public schools, the U.S. Supreme Court, the presidency, the medical system, and churches or organized religion.[32]

When asked, "Which of these industries do you think are generally honest and trustworthy—so that you normally believe a statement by a company in that industry?" fewer than 20 percent of Americans answered positively for the following industries: computer companies, utilities, packaged food companies, life insurance companies, airlines, car manufacturers, pharmaceutical companies, health insurance companies, telecommunication companies, HMOs, social media companies, oil companies, and tobacco companies. Fewer than 10 percent of Americans felt the last five listed were trustworthy.[33]

We are witnessing a wholesale collapse in trust across a range of institutions, which is creating higher and more complicated hurdles for businesses. As a response to this collapse, Americans have become more self-reliant, cynical, and independent. But delegation and cooperation are natural human traits. We have always traded our strengths. It started as something like, "You make butter, I'll make soap, and we'll trade." Of course, you wouldn't have traded your carefully crafted soap for rancid butter, or traded with someone you didn't like or trust. You would have gone back to churning your own butter or sought out a new trading partner.

It's more complicated now. We use money, and we "trade" with far-flung partners. But human nature and the concept of exchange work in exactly the same way. For example, whereas once consumers sought loans from the local bank with an assumption of trust, today all banks (and most businesses) start with worse than a blank slate—they start with a trust deficit. The untrusting consumer scours the Internet for banking partners. Some companies are responding by offering products and services in a completely different way.

In another era, for example, it would have been unheard of for a bank without a building or local branch offices to be successful. But GoBank is an entirely app-fueled bank with no physical presence, no checks or paper, no ATMs of their own—and even in their beta test phase, they were a success. Their pitch is a "pay what you want" membership fee structure—consumers can choose any fee from zero to $9.00 a month—and a warm, casual vibe. Though they're set to make plenty of profit on higher-than-average swipe fees and extremely low overhead (no tellers to employ, no real estate to own, and lower taxes), they offer consumers the perception that they care more about people than profits. In the tone of its communications, GoBank exhibits a human, un-banklike personality complete with puppies and such statements as, "We think everyone should be able to have a GoBank account," and "Pay us whatever you think is fair."

Our belief in innovation and confidence in technology have laid the foundation for the success of GoBank. But because it's very hard to get consumers to break up with their existing banks, the success of GoBank is dependent on one more thing: distrust and disappointment in existing businesses. As San Altman, VP of mobile for Green Dot, GoBank's parent company, said, "If you look at people who have an iPhone or Android and are under 40 and are dissatisfied with their bank, it's actually quite a large market."[34]

Not just in the banking industry, but across the board, the Internet has given people the means to be more self-reliant. And because the scales have tipped away from trust toward vigilance, a broader range of people are choosing "me first." More frequently than ever, consumers tell me about how they use the power of their money and their influence on social media to punish businesses.

"I hate eBay," said Paige, an affluent executive. "My husband used to buy me the most gorgeous shoes—but with four-inch heels. I just can't wear that much heel anymore, so started selling them on eBay. I did this for a few years, and I would get the nicest feedback. People loved the shoes." Paige encountered a dishonest buyer and didn't get the support she expected from eBay. "There are scummy people out there, but what I can't forgive is that eBay and their equally evil partner PayPal just took my money out of my account and gave it to the liar. To make matters worse, their customer service—well, it doesn't exist. There was never a person I could speak with. So now I'm doing all the talking—I warn everyone to stay away from selling on eBay and PayPal too. I had convinced a couple of my friends to weed out their closets and try selling on eBay—you can bet I've told them about my experience, and we're all boycotting eBay. Now we sell on RealReal."

Once it was caveat emptor, but now it's more like caveat venditor—let the seller beware. Hell hath no fury like a scorned shopper. I have heard hundreds of stories from shoppers with the same level of emotional intensity. What's changed in the past few years is what shoppers do about it. They talk—a lot. They post negative reviews. They actively seek out and root for alternatives. Today, they make their opinions known—because they have so many ways they *can* make their opinions known.

It's important to add that this shift is accompanied by ever-diminishing amounts of time and patience. So when people do ignore what they perceive to be a breach of trust, poor service, rudeness, or disappointment, it's not that they don't care—they're simply choosing their battles. But that negative perception lingers, and the tarnished brand or retailer is vulnerable to competition or bad-mouthing at some point.

On the bright side, I hear just as many love stories as I do "bad store" stories. Kevin spent top dollar to purchase a new bicycle from a local high-end boutique. He said that he went back and forth in his mind about paying "a little extra" to purchase it from the shop rather than to buy online. "I wanted to support a local small business, they had exactly what I needed, and then in the end, I just really liked the guy that took care of me, so I bought it there. I have been thrilled, and believe me, I've told everyone."

Similarly, Jesse bought a new iPhone that malfunctioned. "I took it to the genius bar, and after testing it, they just gave me a new one! I was so afraid it would be a runaround." When I asked Jesse if she told anyone else about the experience, she said, "When I posted it on Facebook, there were lots of comments from friends, and most of them were really positive too."

> Shoppers of consumer electronics are three times more likely to pay attention to consumer reviews than to professional reviews.[r]

Consumers *want* to trust. It's in our nature to want to "trade" with confidence—it's easier and faster, and feels better. Because consumers often feel burned, wary, unseen, and disrespected (not just by businesses but for all the reasons covered in the first part of this chapter), the businesses that exhibit compassion, humanity, and personality have a magnificent opportunity to connect—deeply.

A New Fairness Equation: In It for Ourselves

Today's more guarded consumers are not only more self-reliant. They also feel a diminished obligation to be fair. In situations where the bond of trust is weakened, an "everyone for themselves" mentality takes an even firmer hold. Which is a partial explanation for a decrease in the integrity of some consumers when it comes to shopping.

> An exhaustive study conducted by the Association for Psychological Science found two essential ingredients of cooperative communities: (1) high trust in leaders, and (2) a strong sense of identity and belonging within the community.[s]

Although most consumers have maintained a sense of honesty, gray areas of fairness are on the rise, which makes behaviors like wardrobing (the practice of buying, using, and then returning merchandise) and showrooming (scouting out merchandise in a store and then buying it online) more acceptable.

"Every year it gets more extravagant," says Jillian of her son's high school end-of-year parties. "The moms have to outdo each other. So this year a mom bought red leather couches and huge television monitors. And then she returned them all after the event! Nice message to send your kid, huh?" Nick's told everyone about how he "rented" boogie boards in Hawaii for free by buying them at Costco and then returning them when it was time to go home. In another age, you might want to keep that type of dishonesty to yourself; today, it's a source of pride for some to "outfox" retailers.

Shoppers are aware of these transgressions and more wary as a result. "I was considering a gorgeous full-price winter coat at Bloomingdales," recalls Mimi. "While trying it on, I found a tiny salt packet in the pocket. Obviously someone had worn that 'new' coat to the movies. Ick, I was so disgusted. Why don't they put tags or something on the outside of their clothes so that people know they're buying something that hasn't been worn?" Bloomingdales and other stores have recently begun to do just that. In an earlier era of greater trust, consumers might have felt insulted—as if they themselves were being accused of potential dishonesty. Today, consumers are looking for protection and are much less sensitive to retailers' efforts to offer assurances that they're buying unworn merchandise.

Mimi's comment is also a reflection of the fact that consumers have a little quirk about sharing contact of any sort with other consumers. Paco Underhill was first to discover that being touched by a stranger while shopping would shorten time spent in a store. He called it the Butt Brush Factor in his seminal work on consumer behavior, *Why We Buy*.[35] Clearly, as we become more disconnected, the disgust factor of shopping in stores is likely to increase. For example, a recent UK study found that shoppers who were accidentally touched by a stranger had more negative feelings about brands, found products in the store to be less valuable, and spent less time in the store.[36] Incidentally, consumers respond favorably to intentional touches from store employees.

In another study, shoppers discounted the value of new, unworn shirts based on the faulty belief that the shirt had been touched by another shopper. In the study, participants were instructed to try on a $20 shirt. Some participants were directed to a shirt displayed on a regular sales rack; those people rated the value of the shirt to be the full $20. Others were told that the shirt could be found on the return rack; for that group, the value of the shirt dropped to $16.18. A third group was told that the shirt was being tried on right that minute, and that group valued the shirt at only $11.72. We have unconscious beliefs about how products become contaminated by their contact with other products and most especially with other people.[37]

People spend dirty money (not ill gotten, but clearly used and "contaminated" by human contact) more quickly than crisp new bills. For example, research participants spent an average of $3.68

when given a new $20 bill and an average of $8.35 when given a dirty $20 bill.[38]

This "rub-off" effect—whereby products gain characteristics through their contact with other products or people—held true for the value of products as well. When cheaper products are bundled with more expensive products, they often devalue the more elite products. In an experiment involving everything from scooters to home gyms, consumers devalued the more expensive item by approximately 25 percent when it was paired with an inexpensive product.[39]

MARKETING TO THE INDIVIDUALIST CONSUMER

The days when a marketer could rely on demographic profiling are over. In an individualistic society, an "18–24 year old single, Caucasian male" chafes at products and marketing communications that are aimed to satisfy the lowest common denominator of his cohort. Ditto for every age, race, marital status, gender, and geographic subgroup out there.

A more individualistic consumer wants more attention, personalization, involvement, and appreciation. All of this is made possible by one of the very dividers of society—technology. Marketers have both the challenge and the opportunity to build trust, involve, and connect with consumers on a more personal level. Although consumers may never utter these words in a focus group, the truth is that they are yearning to be seen and to trust marketers and retailers. Connection is the emotional driver of our times.

At the very least, marketers and retailers can get a leg up by offering their consumers some relief from a growing sense of invisibility and invisibility's frequent companion, defensiveness. A lack of trust means that consumers are more wary. They need to feel more in control. They search deeper and harder for assurance that they're making smart choices. This assurance often comes in the form of discounts, but it's really not about the money—or at least not only about the money. Discounts signal value, and that's why they've become the vanguard of retail. If consumers had more trust in the value of what they were considering, they'd still love a discount, but they'd also be more willing to pay full price.

Wendy Liebmann, CEO of WSL Strategic Retail, thinks Burberry is one company that has done just that by highlighting why their products are worth their premium prices. "It's not enough to focus on the deal; you need to focus on the value. When Burberry reorganized, they communicated that in good times or bad times, this product is worth it, and they communicated why a product's cost was a value."[40]

After over two decades of devotion to Hermès, Marcia decided that their silk scarves had reached a price point that was "ridiculous." "When they hit the $375 mark, I felt like I would just be a sucker for buying one." Last year, Marcia renewed her relationship with Hermès because of a traveling exhibition of Hermès craftsmanship. "When I saw a scarf actually being made, it became clear to me why they cost over $400. In fact, I think that might actually be a bargain. I bought one that day, and I suppose I'll get back to my schedule of adding one to my collection every six months or so."

Awash with choices and unfettered by the fashion guardrails of previous decades, today's consumers are also more likely to use what they buy and how they shop as a way to communicate and bond with others. Jenny, twenty-eight, describes her mismatched outfit as a hit because "it's more interesting if it doesn't match." People are more likely to notice her, and her eclectic taste is a clue to her personality. The word "interesting" is an interesting choice—it implies that part of Jenny's mission is to choose products that will engage the interest of other people. Similarly, Patsy, fifty-five, who treasures her reputation as the "shopping expert" among her friends, was ecstatic when she nabbed several limited-edition

Missoni pieces during a recent Target-Missoni collaboration: "I totally scored." She purchased pieces for several friends. "I can't wait to surprise them; you can't buy these anywhere now."

Today's consumer is also is more willing, and even expects, to be consulted about products—from the design and functionality of Caterpillar trucks to potato chip flavors. "Pick your favorite" campaigns on Facebook have an astonishing 27 percent response rate.[41]

The partnerships and loyalties consumers once had with brands and retailers are more fragile. The retailers and marketers that succeed truly understand and empathize with their consumers. They help them know that they are genuinely respected and valued, and they help reinforce that consumers are making smart choices by selecting their products and brands. As Liebmann points out, "In a world that's very unsettled—economically, politically, socially, and technologically—trust in a retailer and brand are very, very important."

3

Intensified Emotions

Throughout the world, Americans have a reputation as positive and optimistic people. And we still are, but today quite a few of us are also a bit crankier and slightly more irritable than we have been in the past. Which means that *everyone* is affected. Because even if you're not in a bad mood or stressed-out yourself, you will be after spending the day with people who are. That's not just common sense, but involves a phenomenon psychologists call "emotional contagion." It seems we can even "catch" the bad moods of strangers.[1]

The shifting moods of Americans are critical for marketers to understand. Our moods and emotions have a tremendous impact on how we perceive the world, and that includes our perceptions of brands, products, and retailers. Persistent anxiety and anger, even mild versions, also give people new psychological motivations for buying. We think differently when emotions are in play. Our brain computes values and weighs choices in different ways when we feel stressed-out, anxious, or irritated.

The tiny portion of the brain known as the ventromedial prefrontal cortex is the worrywart center of the brain and a major force in computing the economic value of products. Recent brain imaging studies show that it is also a hotbed of *emotional* calculations—proving what smart marketers have known all along: emotions enter into the appraisal and trade-off functions of buying decisions.[2]

- According to a report issued in 2010, 20 percent of Americans take medications to improve their mental health, which represents a 22 percent increase from 2001 to 2010. More than 10 percent of middle-aged women and nearly 6 percent of middle-aged men take antianxiety medications. The number of teenagers taking antianxiety medications nearly doubled from 2001 to 2010.[a]
- More than half of Americans say they're angry about taxes, unemployment, the government, immigration, the economy, big business, and education.[b]
- Nearly 45 percent of Americans lay awake at night because of stress.[c]
- One-third of Americans say they experience chronic stress at work.[d]
- Barely 53 percent of Americans said they were hopeful about an improvement of their personal circumstances in 2013, and fully 44 percent said they were instead "fearful." A record low of only 40 percent said they were hopeful about the world in general.[e]
- A 1994 survey of randomly selected households found that 15 percent of Americans had experienced elevated anxiety the previous year. Fifteen years later, the percentage had risen to 49.5 percent.[f]

This chapter explains the rise in irritability we're experiencing, including a discussion of the roots of stress, anxiety, anger, and narcissism and of the changes in society that have activated these protective and defensive emotions. As in the previous two chapters, we'll highlight crucial insights for marketers, including how these emotional shifts shape the way people shop—why shoppers have become bargain hungry, how shopping can be therapeutic, and why traditional marketing research is less predictable than ever.

NARCISSISM

Narcissism is a personality style with powerful emotional components that drive interactions and purchasing needs. Most people are not narcissists in a clinical sense of the word, but everyone has some narcissistic qualities. That is, we all exhibit some degree of superficiality, self-focus, a sense of invisibility, emphasis on the individual rather than the group, and high expectations of individual specialness.

A number of factors, including those discussed in the previous two chapters, seem to be increasing our overall societal level of narcissistic thought and behavior:

- Technology has given us a taste for both fast, visual bits of information and put an emphasis on appearances (that is, superficiality).
- We feel less visible and less connected to each other.
- We're more self-focused and self-protective because we sense that we have less common ground with others, and thus trust others less.
- We're affected by the pervasive, self-centered messages of the self-esteem movement.

Narcissism activates particular consumer needs to feel special and appreciated. These are obvious needs that are familiar to marketers. But more subtle factors come into play when we operate out of narcissism: most notably anger and competitiveness. Marketers need to understand the real roots of narcissism both because it's on the rise and because it activates some of our deepest, darkest emotions. Understanding narcissism means better understanding what consumers want and need.

Caroline is exceptionally attractive. She helps along her great genes with facials, trainers, weekly hair appointments, Botox injections and cosmetic surgery, a stylist, and a designer wardrobe. She spends more money on these products and services than she does on her car and apartment combined—without batting a shellacked eyelash. "It's an investment," she says.

Caroline has an MBA from Harvard and describes her job this way: "I'm the number two at a new venture capital firm in Silicon Valley. I work constantly. I know my life doesn't have balance, but what I'm doing is important, and the payoff will be huge." About relationships, she says she doesn't have many friends because "women tend to be threatened by me, or jealous. . . . I've always had better luck with men as friends, but then you have to deal with them hoping you'll have sex with them." Caroline also doesn't have much luck with love. "I am so sick of that inevitable part where they try to tell me how I could be happier or what I need. Like the last guy. We're sitting in a restaurant, and he's trying to tell me that I'm—whatever. I said, 'Did *you* go to Harvard? What do you know about what I need?' I walked out." When asked if she had ever been in love, Caroline says, "The guy before him I thought was the one. He thought I was too intense. I'm glad I found out before we got engaged or married that he couldn't handle a strong woman."

Caroline is what some would call "full of herself." Others might describe her as selfish, grandiose, or narcissistic.

Narcissism exists on a continuum. At one end is a realistic and balanced self-interest along with the desire to grow and improve—but not at the expense of others. At the other end is an unrealistic, inflated sense of self-importance, a lack of empathy for others, the need for constant admiration, and hypersensitivity to criticism. Closer to this end of the continuum, narcissism increasingly interferes with the ability to be vulnerable, honest, and empathic in relationships, and past a certain point it becomes clinically diagnosable.

Subclinical narcissism—the kind every consumer exhibits to some degree—is obviously of the most interest to marketers. But knowing what real narcissism looks like—and what's behind it—is crucial to understanding these drives in all of us. There are two secret giveaways to personalities with a bonus shot of narcissism, like Caroline. First, they tend not to know that they themselves are the source of most of their relationships problems. They're avid blamers instead. Second, they have more contempt for others than most. Why? Contempt is the enemy of empathy and the elevator of the ego. It facilitates a feeling of superiority, and—important but less obvious—it is also a way to jettison a bit of the anger that is the narcissist's common companion.

The flash and arrogance of narcissists is obvious. What's not so obvious is how hard they work to feel worthy of love. What they've learned in life so far is that achieving things, having things, and looking a particular way should earn you love. The version of "love" they know is all about the surface. Getting enough of this kind of love requires lots of self-absorbed work, and that doesn't leave much room to focus on other people and their needs. This typically means that unless someone is in a relationship with a narcissist for their own needs for power, money, or status, the relationship won't last long. Bad as this may be for people trying to be in a relationship with a narcissist, it also leaves narcissists themselves trapped in a nasty perpetual cycle. Their self-centeredness prevents them from acquiring the genuine connections that will relieve their distress; they therefore try even harder to "improve" themselves. And that means they're again focusing on the superficial aspects of themselves, leaving even less room for empathy and interest in others. Like dogs and cats overgrooming themselves when they're anxious, narcissists' obsessiveness about their source of pride—their appearance, financial prowess, or expertise—is a mask and a distraction for anxiety.

The self-centered attitudes and actions of narcissists are caused by emotional distress. Worse, because they typically mask this distress—even to themselves—with assorted dysfunctional actions (like leaving well-intentioned boyfriends at restaurant tables), their emotional vulnerability is easy to dismiss. Anger and contempt are their natural human responses to the anguish of feeling unseen and to the inevitable disappointment that follows entitlement.

- An analysis of popular song lyrics from 1987 to 2007 found an increase in self-referential lyrics and a decrease in lyrics related to social interactions. In addition, lyrics in the 2000s became more negative, angry, and combative than the happier, connection-focused lyrics of the late 1980s.[3]
- The average middle-class American household has eighty-five pictures of themselves and their pets on display.[4]
- In 1950, 12 percent of teens said they thought they were "an important person." In the late 1980s, nearly 80 percent of teens endorsed that statement.[5]
- In the 1960s, the average Academy Awards acceptance speech was forty seconds long. Today, it averages two minutes.[6]
- Nearly 60 percent of adults 18–34 would rather stand out than blend into a crowd. For adults 35–49, only 36 percent prefer to stand out, and fewer than 30 percent of adults 50–64 prefer to stand out.[7]

Standing out, feeling important, and enjoying pictures of your family are all fine—until they morph into self-absorption that interferes with the essential human tasks of caring for and helping other people.

Secret Narcissists

There are loads of seemingly caring, even altruistic people who are actually motivated by hidden narcissism. Beneath a veneer of passionate caring lies their primary goal—admiration, power, and the opportunity to vent their personal rage.

Pamela is one of these people. She sounds compassionate, engaged, and smart when she vigorously berates a wide assortment of "they's" who are destroying the (that is, her) world. Her contempt is unleashed with tirades against big business, the rich, polluters, fur wearers, and anyone who disagrees with her. When Pamela is spouting off, she comes alive and clearly feels virtuous, energized, and powerful. Pamela is what we'd call a closet narcissist, someone who has perfected the appearance of a caring and selfless person. But if you peel back a thin outer layer, what you find is someone who dominates conversations, spreads her contempt and blame far and wide, lacks empathy for the "they's" out there, and has an entirely inflated sense of herself and her opinions.

Another hidden form of narcissism—one I call "narcissism by proxy"—is evident in some parental behavior. I encountered it when I was a guest on Ronn Owens's popular call-in talk show, discussing Generation Y. A caller was concerned about what he described as a lack of civility among young people. To demonstrate his point, he relayed a story about college students sitting on a sidewalk with their legs outstretched, ignoring the fact that passersby had to walk into the street to get around them. The next caller was the mother of a Gen Y girl who called to defend the generation. As she talked, she became angrier and angrier. Ronn Owens pointed out the comment of the previous caller, and she responded by spitting out, "Why should my daughter have to get out of anyone's way?" The caller was using her daughter as a proxy to vent and express her own sense of entitlement. But notice the out-of-proportion anger: it's similar to Caroline's walking out on her boyfriend in a restaurant.

We're likely to see this trend continue, because narcissism begets more narcissism. People offended by the selfish actions of others will become more self-focused and self-protective—which means they're also contributing to the invisibility that other people feel when they're in public, in turn spurring them to work harder to be seen and admired. And if everyone is a leader, who is following? If everyone is scrambling for attention and admiration, who is doing the admiring?

Twitter is often uncharitably said to be perfect for our narcissistic age. It enables people to gather followers, talk all about themselves, all without having to listen to anyone.
—Jeremy Dean[8]

Narcissism Goes Shopping

With narcissism on the rise, and knowing that to some extent narcissism exists in all of us, marketers would be wise to harness the allure of specialness, exclusivity, secrets, and social ranking systems.

Special and exclusive offerings are like catnip to the narcissistically oriented. It's not just about getting; it's about winning. As James was admiring a Zegna suit at Nordstrom, his regular sales associate leaned in close and whispered, "I can't believe it, but those are actually on sale." James expressed surprise. The sales associate replied in a hushed whisper, "I know! Those basics never go on sale! It's a secret though. See? We don't even have them marked." James bought the suit on the spot.

Secrets are exciting, and they create a bond. They work not just for the more narcissistic shopper—all of us feel special when we're on the "inside." Fast-food restaurant In-N-Out Burger has a "secret" menu that includes "animal-style" fries that are loaded with onions, cheese, and a secret sauce. They also have a grilled cheese sandwich that's not on their regular menu. Only those "in the know" can order them, and it creates a bond and furthers the cult status of In-N-Out among their fans. The allure of secret knowledge explains the success of another tactic that Nordstrom uses effectively: "early access" to their anniversary sale for Nordstrom credit card holders. Upcoming sale merchandise is displayed behind translucent curtains in stores. Really anyone can gain entry, but it feels exclusive and therefore special and more exciting to shoppers.

Early access to sale merchandise and exclusive coveted offerings for Facebook fans, special customers, and Twitter followers are "wins" that bond consumers to a retailer or brand. Knowing that other people wanted what you got turns a product into prize. Limited offerings and private events become more coveted when they're secretly or personally offered early to an exclusive set of customers. Even a coffee mug can become more desirable with exclusivity. Researchers found that participants were three times more likely to buy a coffee mug when they were told that they were randomly selected to receive a special discount.[9]

Our narcissistically induced cravings for "specialness" offer insight into why multilevel loyalty programs work much better than dual-level programs: they activate social ranking. A study published in the *Journal of Consumer Research* found that regardless of where an individual would be ranked, people overwhelmingly preferred three-tier status programs to two-tier programs.[10] "In or out" isn't as satisfying as "high, higher, and highest."

We all want to feel special, but those with stronger narcissistic tendencies have an even greater interest in products that are exclusive, customizable, or personalizable. According to professor Russell Seidle of McGill University, coauthor of a study on product scarcity, "Narcissistic consumers demonstrate a preference for scarce products that correspond with their views of themselves as unique individuals. Scarcity in and of itself seems to be the main driver of their purchasing behavior."[11]

Luxury retailers have long known the allure of exclusivity. That allure sounds something like, "I must be a rare and special person to own such a rare and special product." As narcissism gains a stronger foothold in the psyches of American consumers, special offerings and events take on even greater significance. The requisite "secret handshake" signifies to consumers that they're seen and honored and that their specialness has been duly noted. Opportunities to meet designers, attend star-studded events or fashion shows, or gain entry behind the scenes flatter and engage consumers. Gucci takes their top customers to the Cannes Film Festival, American Express provides private airport lounges to their top cardholders, and Nordstrom lets credit card holders behind the "translucent screen."

Specialness is at a premium in another way now. In a world where everything feels available to everyone anytime, the old-fashioned thrill of finding something special, unique, and exclusive is more appealing than ever. A rare find, much like a private invitation or exclusive offering, bonds consumers to a retailer or brand. When I interview consumers, I typically ask them to tell me about a recent purchase that was particularly exciting. More than ever, I hear about something they thought was unique or rare. One woman was thrilled to bring Wine Gums home from Canada because "they're like special gummy bears that you can't get here." Another told me about a lava lamp that not only reminded him of his college years but also was something he had never seen in a store before. Another interviewee mentioned a pair of hand-made shoes that she was sure she wouldn't see anyone else wearing. These products are memorable because they're unique, and in a world where you can get literally anything in the world, exclusivity is prized.

Narcissism and the Critical Customer

As I mentioned earlier, narcissism is characterized by increased sensitivity to disrespect. It also unleashes blaming and vengeance. Woe is the retailer or brand that is the target of a narcissist's rage: narcissists may be a small minority of customers (and it's essential to protect your perception of your customers by keeping that in mind), but social media and other technology can potentiate their anger like never before, sowing incivility and bad feelings into many conversations about the brand or retailer.

The key to understanding the difference between the honest criticism of a customer and the wounded outcry of a narcissist is in the tone. As you've probably guessed already, the narcissist's anger is likely to be out of proportion to the incident. That's because it's usually not the incident but a presumption of disrespect that has inflamed the situation. Keeping that deeper motivation in mind is the key to quick resolution.

One of the biggest opportunities that retailers have is in recognizing that consumers are more angry and anxious, and asking themselves, "How can I help?" It's in the solution where you start to build value and loyalty.
—Wendy Liebmann[12]

How you respond to angry customers, no matter their level of narcissism, will affect how they respond. Your confidence is key because *defensiveness implies guilt* and offers a justification for their anger. It's essential that you start with a mind-set of confidence, calm, and caring—you, not your customers, set the tone. Their behavior might feel like a personal attack, but it's not personal. It's more about them than it is about you. Every single consumer I've interviewed has stories about disrespectful and inept customer service, and many, particularly narcissists, enter the conversation angry not just about the current incident but about previous encounters.

Taking a nondefensive, confident attitude also means that you receive problems with gratitude. Complaints are free research and simply information. Yes, it's really hard to respond to anger with calm, but looking at the encounter from the perspective of information or research helps. It also makes it easier to listen carefully and empathically, which is the essential secret solution to deflating narcissistic rage.

The more narcissistic the customer, the less interested she will be in understanding the reasons the problem occurred (the brand's point of view) and the more interested she will be in hearing that her inconvenience or concerns are recognized and significant. One women I spoke with said her anger turned to mush when the customer service representative she was speaking with on the phone blurted out, "Oh no—that's awful!" "He regained composure and went back to the bullshit script of 'I apologize for the inconvenience,' but it was too late. I saw that as a human being he cared, and I just couldn't be angry anymore."

Of course this type of caring is in addition to the traditional five steps of apologizing: hearing the problem, acknowledging the impact of the loss, sincerely apologizing, offering amends, and providing assurance or proof that the problem won't happen again.

Increasingly, these conversations between critical customers and brands or retailers are happening in public, online. Monitoring and responding to negative online feedback and reviews are essential. In these cases, responding, rather than reacting, and demonstrating confidence and caring are the foundation of a positive outcome. When businesses respond to negative reviews, more than one-third of reviewers will delete their review, and another third will repost a positive one.[13] Companies that make mistakes and apologize are actually rated higher than they were before they made the error. Consumers don't just want to have the mistake fixed; they want to feel seen and respected. Early "intervention" prevents festering, and it speaks volumes to potential customers who read reviews.

Here's an example from Amazon:

> I have changed my rating from 1 to 5. I would like to inform everyone buying from Pintoli that they are an

exceptional vendor. They read my 1 star review and soon after sent me a letter that informed me that they understood my dissatisfaction with their 1066 men's compression socks as to the improper sizing provided on the site. They were nice enough to send me free of charge a XXL size 1066. Now that is a business who wishes to satisfy their customers. They make a great compression sock and they back up their product too. I will continue to buy their product with confidence!

THE MARKETER'S MINI PRIMER ON THE PSYCHOLOGY OF STRESS, ANXIETY, AND ANGER

Though we like to think of ourselves as rational shoppers, when emotions enter the equation we respond differently to marketing cues, have different needs and motivations for buying, and evaluate retailers and our purchases differently. Even low levels of stress, anxiety, and anger—so low that shoppers barely register their impact—siphon resources from cognitive to physical functions. As shoppers approach the marketplace with greater levels of emotionality, marketers are wise to understand the impact of these emotions on consumers.

This Is Your Brain on Stress

A fundamental truth of human psychology is that change of any sort is stressful. Even happy changes like weddings and babies stress our emotional resources because they require adaptation and attention. More difficult changes and, especially, unexpected ones obviously compound the effects of stress. And we have all experienced change—sometimes massive changes—in the past few years.

In the right doses, stress brings out the best in us—it's inspiring and invigorating. Besides, the alternative would be a completely uneventful and deathly boring life. But stress is also the common denominator of all emotional disorders, and stress reduction is part of any strategy for improving mental health.

As you would expect, overall stress levels are on the rise. This is a shift that affects all shoppers, but some more than others. In a grocery shopping study that I conducted, I found three factors that are nearly perfect predictors of "stress shopping": financial resources, time, and emotional support. Large deficits in any one category or smaller dips across two or three categories create a stress-shopping mentality. For example, wealthy consumers without supportive friends or family and with limited time shop similarly to financially strapped consumers with more relaxed schedules and family help.

> Nearly two-thirds of parents say they're stressed-out about back-to-school shopping. Time constraints are named as the number-one source of stress.[g]

Tiffany is a married thirty-one-year-old stay-at-home mom of two. She and her husband own their small home in Charlotte. It's a jumble of toys, in-progress scrapbooks, and laundry waiting to be folded. Money is very tight, and Tiffany says that she worries constantly about making ends meet. She plans her weekly meals around whatever meat is on sale at the grocery store. She's a big fan of the Food Network, which plays in the background when she's at home. Her recipes are either old family favorites or something she picked up on the Food Network.

Because Tiffany shops with her children, she moves quickly through the store. She typically purchases without brand loyalty and according to the yellow sale tags on the shelf. There are a few exceptions: she selected Montreal Seasoning because Rachel Ray recommended it, Kraft cheese because she "just likes" the brand, and Del Monte tomatoes because she was able to quickly locate the cut and flavor she needed. Toward the end of one shopping trip, she impulsively added a box of full-priced Rice Krispies Treats saying that because she'd been so bargain conscious, she could give herself and her kids a treat. According to my quick grocery cart calculations, the price of the Rice Krispies Treats ate up over half of the nickels and dimes she'd saved by gravitating toward those yellow sale markers during this shopping trip.

Tiffany's shopping trip demonstrates a few of the ways that brands break through when stress runs high: through associations with trusted experts or friends; through long-term, consistently replenished brand relationships; and by making shopping easier. Tactics discussed later in this book such as the use of cross-promotions, semiotics, the "rub-off" effect, and authenticity all contribute to a brand that breaks through when stress runs high.

* * *

Even mild levels of stress affect which parts of the brain are used in decision making. Under normal conditions, we use the hippocampus, which is associated with making decisions through a conscious, deliberate strategy. Stress causes people to use the midbrain, which is associated with unconscious learning and "gut" feelings. This means that today, consumers are more likely than ever to be swayed by emotion rather than logic. It's also a partial explanation for why consumers seem to be so bad at math. It's not that they are innumerate; it's more that they're using parts of their brains that are more emotionally focused and not so great with the details.

Symbols and cues have a lot to do with how shoppers perceive prices when emotions are in play. Arbitrary numbers set "anchors" that guide our behavior and our perception of what's appropriate. Therefore, for example, the first offer in a salary negotiation becomes the figure against which we measure our success. And a few high-priced goods in a store can make less expensive price tags on more modest items seem like a bargain. When Williams-Sonoma placed a $429 bread maker near a $279 model, they didn't sell many of the more expensive bread makers, but sales of the $279 model doubled. It seemed like a great deal next to the anchor of the $429 model.[14] Similarly, when limits are put on the number of products a person can buy, they unconsciously cue shoppers that that's the appropriate quantity to purchase. People are much more likely to buy four cans of soup than two cans of soup when they are told there is a four-can limit.[15]

Another cue is the number 9, which is strongly associated with discounted and bargain prices. Multiple studies have shown that people think that products ending with the number 9 are a better deal. Of course, it also discounts the value of the product. For example, a full-priced luxury item priced at $6,799 would be perceived to be discounted and consequently less valuable than the same product priced at $6,750.

We also tend to judge probabilities based on how often we hear of examples. This explains why people worry about shark attacks when they're incredibly unlikely. We're twice as likely to be killed by an alligator as by a shark and over ten times more likely to be hit by lightning. This also explains why people play the lottery.

Of course, there are also consumers who are simply poor at math, or they don't have the focus or time to go through the process of calculating a 20 percent discount or a cost per ounce.

Beyond their having math problems, I've found that stressed-out shoppers behave differently compared to relatively unstressed shoppers in these ways:

- They are more prone to inertia—buying the same thing without thinking, or not buying at all.
- They rely more heavily on trusted experts, such as bloggers, cooking programs, friends, or favorite stores to curate and whittle down what they consider to be excessive options. They

gravitate toward smaller pools of options and appreciate help getting there.

- They are more likely to rationalize impulsive purchases.
- They are less deliberate in their decision making and rely more on in-store feelings and symbolic cues to make decisions.
- They are highly sensitive to complexity—if it's not simple, they're not buying. Likewise, they feel grateful and are loyal to brands and retailers that organize and simplify the buying process.

Edgy and Anxious

Anxiety, the cousin of stress, is the self on high alert. Like stress, a little bit of anxiety serves a purpose. It heightens our senses, prepares us for action, and helps us avoid disaster. Anxiety in small doses is motivation's little helper emotion—just the jolt needed to get us to try harder, make changes, stay alert, or be creative. Anxiety in larger or longer doses can often mean a heart attack—literally.

The antidote to anxiety is control. When people feel they have control—even if it's just the control that comes from knowing when something disastrous will happen—they'll feel less anxious. People who are anxious often don't *feel* jumpy; they might instead be vexed by perfectionism, blaming, or obsessiveness. All three are psychological tricks our minds use to feel more in control.

Simply uttering a phrase that reinforces control results in happier, more confident consumers—who are then also twice as likely to accept a request. "It's your decision," "you're free to choose," "don't feel obligated," and so forth all work. This is much more effective in face-to-face communication, but still somewhat effective in email communication. Activating a person's sense of control makes him or her more open to persuasion.[h]

Anxiety shows itself in various shopping behaviors: bargain hunting that's in good part simply a quest for assured value; use of the ratings and reviews of other shoppers, which are more trusted than retailers; and online shopping for mental relief and distraction. Wary shoppers will combat anxiety by looking for ways to feel more self-reliant and in control.

Anxiety turns hassles and any impediment to purchase into deal breakers. Increased levels of societal anxiety are part of why consumers are more smitten than ever with companies that make shopping and buying easy. "Control" comes in the form of retailer and brand reliability. Psychological research shows that the details of everyday life are a greater predictor of happiness than overall life circumstances.[16] In the same way, seamless, stress-free, hassle-free, confident purchasing is increasingly more satisfying than the splashy thrill of a big complicated purchase.

Hundreds of shoppers have shared with me the emotional intensity they feel around the hassles of shopping:

> I ordered some furniture and had to call four times to find out when it would be delivered. The final blow was when they told me that the reason they had been slow in arranging deliveries was because so many of their customers had entered their phone numbers incorrectly. How insulting. They've got all these customers that can enter their credit card numbers correctly but not their phone numbers?

> I shop online for everything. I mean everything—shoes, light bulbs, dog food, mascara, you name it. Why? Because I'm so tired of going to a store and finding what I need out of stock.

> I just can't stand it when websites fail. You have to enter information more than once or it poops out when you

hit the order button. One mistake and I'm out. (A) It's my credit card so I'm not taking any chances on a cheap operation, and (B) it's just so exasperating.

I have to bring my own bags to the grocery store, schlep my own luggage on the plane, pump gas, pick up my order. It's a self-service world today. Isn't that like saying it's a no-service world today? I always remember when I get good service. It's so rare and so wonderful.

Other shoppers' stories demonstrate that there's a big opportunity for retailers who focus on taking the hassles out of shopping:

I forgot to enter a discount code and called Saks' customer service line, and the woman was not only efficient and effective—she couldn't have been more pleasant. To be honest, I've come to expect hassles, so when I get great service I'm nearly shocked and I'm so grateful.

I am in love with my credit card company. They facilitated my enrollment in an airport security check program that I didn't even know existed. I was thinking of canceling that credit card because of the annual fee, but now I'm their biggest fan. They were looking out for me.

I really love Trader Joe's; you know why? Because I don't have to worry about if I'm being overcharged. I feel like they are working hard to get me good prices. Plus I can get in and out pretty quickly. I like the smaller size.

> After I bought my computer at Apple, they set the
> whole thing up for me right there. I think they really get
> it—I'm not impressed by any computer; what impresses
> me is what it does for me. I left there ready to go.

As these remarks show, simplicity through clarity is beloved by consumers. Intuitively understanding products, store and website layouts, and checkout procedures reduces anxiety. Shoppers tell me that they're often confused about things like sale prices, product locations, and dressing room policies. And when they are, they're more likely to leave than to try to figure things out.

They also want to feel as though their shopping experience was designed around their needs. Jasmine is nearly six feet tall, wears a size large, and has a few words to say about clothing displays. "Tell me why I'm bent in half looking for my size on the bottom shelf when some five-foot-tall girl is on tiptoes trying to get to the small sizes on the top shelf. Just because in somebody's mind it goes small, medium, large doesn't mean they should be displayed that way."

Taking clarity a step further, structure and order remove chaos from the equation and are more inviting to consumers. For example, boundaries around merchandise categories, areas in a store, and even around signage and logos that offer a sense of control are preferred by consumers under stress.[17]

Toronto's Teatro Verde has nailed it in this category. There are multiple small rooms and abundant coordinated content and color themes. There is something amusing, something useful, something adorable in every nook and cranny. It's a contained and comfortable treasure hunt. Owner Shawn Gibson says that none of this is by accident. "We offer a well thought out plan of merchandising. The entrance is stimulating and makes you want to investigate further. There's a fine balance between abundance and organization. Too much abundance, and you can't see the forest for the trees. Too much organization can kill the hunting instinct. We found that offering different contained experiences throughout the store intrigues the consumer and makes them excited to see more."

It's no surprise that Teatro Verde has won Canadian Retailer of the Year. As Gibson points out, "I hear over and over from so many customers that the store makes them feel comfortable and serene."[18]

Ticked Off and Angry

Anger is a common side effect of anxiety, as we saw from the shopper comments quoted earlier. It's also an emotion in its own right— and a sneaky one at that. It looks big and tough, but it's really a mask to hide disappointment, vulnerability, and anguish. It's our mind's way of helping us avoid sadness or shame by marshaling our power against a target, which is why anger sometimes distorts logical thinking. If necessary, the brain will sacrifice rationality in order to maintain the self-righteousness and superiority necessary to do battle (and avoid feeling bad). Anger is also dangerous because the targets of anger are often fungible. In other words, someone can be angry that he is disrespected at work or feel generally unloved and turn that into a full-tilt campaign against a company that he feels has disrespected or disregarded him. The company can become a target for the discharged anguish a person has felt in other realms. This discharge of emotion can trump fairness, and it's a phenomenon marketers will find themselves contending with from increasingly irritable consumers.

There are plenty of reasons why people are angry today—many of them discussed in the previous chapter. But one that's often overlooked is the connective power of anger. Nothing unites us like a common enemy, and plenty of people are looking for a way to belong. And for those suffering from the side effects of technology, such as a sense of invisibility or emotional detachment, anger is an easy route to passion and power. Tim Kreider expertly sums up some of this freewheeling anger in his book *We Learn Nothing*: "So many letters to the editor and comments on the Internet have the same tone of thrilled vindication: these are people who have been vigilantly on the lookout for something to be offended by, and found it."[19]

How else to account for the recent Haight-Ashbury "bacon war"? Bacon Bacon is a popular restaurant that serves things like bacon bouquets (which are really just fistfuls of bacon) and bacon caramel corn. Their constantly sold-out T-shirt reads, "You Had Me At Bacon." San Francisco's health department shut them down for several weeks after a few local residents objected to the odor. Turns out that even though bacon smells great when it's cooking, leftover bacon by-products smell like wet cardboard—or worse. A community campaign to protest the closing started with good humor and lots of great punch lines like "Smell This!" and "Really? You complained to the cops that you smelled bacon?" It devolved into threats against the neighbors who complained. The sense of unification and belonging that people are craving and that often arises out of brand love was on full display here. So was the connecting power of anger. (Bacon Bacon reopened after agreeing to some renovations and amendments about where they cook some of their products.)

The energizing, bonding sense of control and power in being "anti" is also part of the reason why consumers are eager to champion the little guy and the more humble retailers and brands that appear to need, want, and appreciate them—to the detriment of older, established retailers.

Anger is the enemy of fairness and rationality. Shoppers in a miffed state of mind are more likely to violate the unspoken rules of fair exchange. Take Linda, who often returns merchandise she's used and leaves clothing she's tried on in a bunch on the dressing room floor. Linda says she feels as though the world has been unfair to her, and she "doesn't care" about being "polite" anymore. Although most shoppers aren't Lindas, many approach the marketplace with an edge. They're more vulnerable and more reactive to perceived slights of any sort.

WHY CONSUMERS ARE MORE EMOTIONAL

Stress. Anxiety. Anger. These emotional states are on the rise. Why? Some of the reasons are related to ubiquitous technology and the rise of individualism:

- Eroding trust in government, businesses, and the media puts the burden of vigilance on our own shoulders and, along with that, more anxiety.
- Our best means of relieving anger and anxiety is through the support and empathy of others, but we have less face-to-face contact and social support today.
- Technology-enabled social comparison can contribute to negative feelings, competitiveness, and the fear of missing out.

I've identified an additional five strong reasons why we're more emotional today:

- Bad news is worse today—because of how we get it.
- The velocity of change makes the world even more unpredictable.
- There is such a thing as too much choice.
- The self-esteem movement has raised our expectations.
- Our happiness expectations are making us unhappy.

Bad News Is Worse Today—Because of How We Get It

We've been pummeled for several years by news that profoundly affects our sense of security in the world, most notably news about the economy, political battles, climate change, and global terrorism. News of all kinds, from wars to entertainment, is also reported in a more sensationalized manner, driven by a news cycle that never lets up for a single minute.

Compounding the effect of the news itself is the way we consume it: all day, every day, in drips and bits through our technology-enabled constant connection to assorted media. A decade ago, most people got their news once or twice a day in a great big deep dive, usually from the morning paper or the evening news.

The drip-and-bit method means that we process news differently in two ways: we never escape it, and we don't get adequate details and analysis. This impairs our ability to deal with the flood of information. Our ability to "compartmentalize" problems, sequestering them until we can give them our attention, is a proven anxiety reducer. So is the sense of predictability that comes from understanding problems. But the way we get news today takes both of these coping mechanisms away and ups our emotional reaction.

The Velocity of Change Makes the World Even More Unpredictable

As I've mentioned, predictability soothes anxiety. Today, the future feels more unpredictable than ever because it comes at us so much faster. We have less time to read and mull, less time to prepare, and less time to adjust. From stock market fluctuations to the knowledge that your television set is "ancient" technology two years after you've bought it—it's a fast-paced world.

No matter how wonderful our options or how bright the future—simply not knowing is stressful. People will go to great lengths to avoid anxiety's fuel: uncertainty. They'll often choose less desirable but certain options over more unpredictable but better options just to know what's coming. And even a future disaster, such as losing a job, feels better if we know when, why, and how.

Some of the most anxiety-provoking changes involve employment. As Jaron Lanier points out in his book *Who Owns the Future?* technology is eating away at the middle class by eroding job security and economic stability. Apps are replacing workers and displacing jobs. And if you have a job, you're working harder than ever, using your smartphone to work around the clock and putting in more hours than ever. Americans clock nearly four hundred hours a year more than their hard-working German counterparts.[20]

There Is Such a Thing as Too Much Choice

We treasure our freedom to choose. We love having abundant choice. At the same time, choice requires thought and mental calculations. That's easy if we have only a few options or are required to make only a few choices a day. But today people struggle with massive numbers of choices, from huge ones (baby, or not?) to small ones (organic, or not?). The strain of choosing (which is really the strain of anticipating living with the consequences of our choices) contributes to chronic, low-level anxiety.

"Sometimes I think I'd rather have my mom's life," says Annie, a thirty-nine-year-old married radio producer with a two-year-old son, Jacob.

> Not really; I mean, she was a housewife, and my dad left her for a younger woman. A cliché if there ever was one. She didn't go to college, and she didn't really have a lot of choices. But still, I remember her playing bridge with the other moms and sharing recipes, and it seems so simple and great compared to the chaos that is my life. I don't have time to ever cook from scratch let alone share recipes. I rarely see my husband. I don't know if I'm making the right choices about my life sometimes. And there is so much to worry about with Jacob. God, everything is something that could hurt him for life— using my iPad, getting vaccinations. I have a beautiful kid, a home, a husband, a job I like. I should be happier—it just seems so hard, and I feel like the bottom could fall out any minute.

Annie describes a scenario that's not uncommon. Although she appreciates being able to choose the kind of life she wants, at the same time she also feels the burden of owning the consequences of those choices. Our youngest adult generations in particular are carving out entirely new ways of living and parenting. That's a lot of scaffolding to construct, and it's no wonder that people like Annie look wistfully on the days of prescribed roles and narrower guardrails—not that anyone would prefer less choice, but many would prefer less complexity and fewer decisions to make. Too much choice + high expectations + an unwritten rule book = anxiety.

From the world of consumer psychology, here are three counterintuitive side effects of abundant choice.

The More = Perfection Mistake

People tend to be happier with what they choose when there are fewer options. When there are lots of choices, we tend to assume there is a perfect match for us, even though it's more likely that all of our choices are similarly "good" and none are perfect. But our assumption that there is one perfect choice among abundant choices can lead to post-purchase dissatisfaction. In an illustration of this concept, researchers asked participants to select one piece of chocolate from a large tray. They then covered the tray for some participants and not for others. Those who were forced to live with their choice (the covered-tray group) were significantly happier with their selection than the group that didn't experience "closure" in their decision.[21]

I feel like I'm a commodity. Like I'm being evaluated against the possibility of somebody that's perfect. I might do that a little too. It's hard to settle when there's always another guy to meet.

—Alicia, 32, on trying online dating for the first time after the breakup of a six-year relationship

---

The Bedeviling Fear of Loss and Regret

It's a human tendency to judge ourselves not by where we are but by where we could have been. The fear of regret not only keeps people sober at business parties but also holds great sway over our purchasing decisions. In a classic experiment conducted by Nobel laureate Daniel Kahneman, winning $100 was found to be half as appealing as losing $100 is *un*appealing.[22] In a similar vein, participants in a research study were given a lottery ticket and then asked if they would trade their ticket for a different one with an equal chance of winning. Fewer than half of the participants agreed— even when they were bribed by chocolate. When the experiment was repeated with pens instead of lottery tickets, 90 percent of participants agreed to trade.[23] People hang on to those lottery tickets in order to avoid the regret they'd experience if they were to switch and their original ticket won. From a marketing perspective, it makes sense that if you give someone $100 to be applied toward a future purchase, she'll find this a greater incentive than a $100 discount.

Our aversion to loss is hardwired. We learn faster from pain than pleasure because negative stimuli get more attention and processing—avoiding loss has kept us alive. It's better to think there is a tiger in the bushes when there isn't one than to think there is no tiger in the bushes when there is one. You can make the first mistake a hundred times, but the second mistake only once. According to Vladas Griskevicius, coauthor of *The Rational Animal*, "we're genetically designed for survival, not quality of life."[24]

The Choice Paralysis Effect

In one of the most well known consumer psychology experiments of the past decade, researcher Sheena Iyengar set up a jam sampling stand in a grocery store. In one version of the experiment, twenty-four jams were offered, in the other only six. Fully 60 percent of customers visited the large assortment of jams compared with only

40 percent who stopped by the smaller assortment. Of those who sampled from the six-jam assortment, 30 percent decided to buy the jam. Of the people who stopped by the large assortment, only 3 percent made a purchase.[25]

The only thing more abundant than the number of choices people need to make today is the quantity of options available to satisfy those choices. The Internet has given every purchase the opportunity to be a multipronged decision campaign. The anxiety of potential regret and the stress of a greater number of mental calculations combine to elevate the emotionality of shoppers. They are entering the marketplace, be it online or in stores, already overloaded.

The Self-Esteem Movement Has Raised Our Expectations

In several of the interviews I conducted for my first book, *Gen BuY*, an interesting phenomenon surfaced. Young, healthy, attractive, articulate adults with interesting jobs—everything you'd hope for someone—were mysteriously anxious. "How do you know when you're making the right choice, if it's good enough?" asked Dale, a successful twenty-nine-year-old designer. Kendra, also twenty-nine and also quite accomplished, added, "When you're told not to settle, that you can do anything, how do you know when what you're doing is good enough?"

The self-esteem movement, full of platitudes like "reach for the stars," "you can do anything," "never settle," and "you're special," was aimed at children, but the message permeated society. As a result, we all have higher expectations about what's expected of us and even higher expectations about what we deserve. Many wonder if the jobs, products, and even relationships they've chosen are "good enough." And for many of the young adults whom I interviewed, "ordinary" was failing. That's stressful.

The self-esteem movement put a lot of emphasis on the self. Social themes that would have at one time seemed indulgent or self-centered are now more resonant: finding yourself, knowing yourself, being yourself. It's not that these are new ideas or bad ideas, but at one time—not so long ago—self-knowledge came through living; it was not a singular pursuit. Or it was a luxury reserved for those who weren't otherwise occupied working, raising children, or serving their communities. Introspection is wonderful, but today self-absorption is an increasingly large part of the curriculum of life, and without balance it leads to anxiety or anger.

Our Happiness Expectations Are Making Us Unhappy

The self-esteem movement, political and marketing messages built on our right to happiness, and a steady stream of self-help books have all fed our current obsession with personal happiness. Along the way, we seem to have forgotten that although the *pursuit* of happiness is psychologically healthy, *expectations* of happiness and feeling entitled to happiness typically have the opposite effect.

The word "happiness" would lose its meaning if it were not balanced by sadness.

—Carl Jung

Why? Because when we feel entitled, we're rarely grateful. And gratitude has been positively correlated with mountains of goodies, including better sleep, stronger immune systems, higher pay, more social connections, more energy, fewer colds—and *happiness*. Further, those who feel entitled to happiness will be more disappointed by the actual ups and downs of life—which leads to anger and resentment.

Yale psychologist Jane Gruber attributes the negative outcomes common to self-help happiness seekers to this: "When you're doing it with the motivation or expectation that these things ought to make you happy, that can lead to disappointment and decreased happiness."[26] Further, as many a great philosopher has pointed out, happiness isn't an ending. The pleasure is in the pursuit. This runs counter to our new quick-fix mentality and the "happy life" social media comparisons mentioned in earlier chapters. We're impatient for happiness, and our expectations are high.

Last, the more focused we are on achieving happiness, the less likely we are to be paying attention to the moments and opportunities that actually make life happy. That's when being happy *with* your life starts to take precedence over being happy *in* your life—when self-evaluation becomes more important than experiences and connecting with other people.

The good life, as I conceive it, is a happy life. I do not mean that if you are good you will be happy; I mean that if you are happy you will be good.

—Bertrand Russell

WHAT THE EMOTIONAL CONSUMER WANTS

Whether they are anxious, stressed, or narcissistically angry, consumers are shopping with more emotion in play. Because of this, they'll gravitate toward purchasing decisions that

- Make them feel more in control
- Reduce the fear of making a mistake
- Simplify the decision process
- Offer clear and immediate emotional benefits
- Are freer of obstacles

Many shoppers use bargains as a way to satisfy all of these needs—to feel more in control and confident about their purchases.

More than three-quarters of women say they're bargain hunters. Fully 90 percent like to tell others about great bargains (and 19 percent even lie about them).[i]

The Allure of the Bargain

Sale! It seems to be the magic word in retail today. Retailers constantly tell me that they hope to wean consumers off of discounting. Understanding why bargains are so satisfying to consumers is the start to wooing consumers without discounts. It's really not (just) about the money. Bargains satisfy not just emotional consumers' needs for control and confidence but also many of their wants. Consumers want to save money, but in my research I've found that discounts and bargains are psychologically potent for eight additional reasons.

FOMO: Fear of Missing Out

Bargain pricing carries a perception that there are limited quantities or that there is a limited period of time to purchase. Inspired by competition or the fear of missing out, shoppers find the inspiration to act *now*. Alexander admits to having a bit of a "shoe thing." "Did I need to buy these? No," he says of the Ted Baker shoes he's just purchased for 50 percent off. "But there's no way they'll be there tomorrow. I had to get them."

Rationalization

Consumers use bargains for psychological permission to buy. Sales allow shoppers to cave in to tempting purchases they might otherwise regret and still see themselves in a positive light. Selina promised herself she would pay off at least half of her credit card balance before adding to her already overstuffed closet. But when she saw that "the cutest" skirt was on sale at Banana Republic, she went for it. "It really wasn't that much; it was on sale. It would have been gone later, and it wasn't much more than I'd pay for dinner," she says.

Managing Option Overload

Many shoppers feel overwhelmed by the quantity of choices available and make a beeline to the sale rack or sale tab to pare down choices and feel more in control.

The Sale "Buzz"

Shoppers who score bargains get a dopamine rush that just plain makes them feel good—and it can be addictive.[27] Lauren half-jokingly says she gets "a rush" when she hears the UPS truck coming down the street. "I have six or seven websites that I check for sales every morning while I'm having my coffee. At least half the time I hear that UPS truck, he's coming to my house. And he's bringing me something I got for a great deal."

The Ben Franklin Syndrome

With so much emphasis on saving, money spent is easy to overlook. Sales make us feel as though we're saving rather than spending. Bradley, thirty-six, recalls his wife returning home from a shopping trip positively giddy with delight at the great sales she'd found at the mall. "I kept asking her how much she'd spent and she didn't have any idea, but she knew exactly how much she'd 'saved.'" Similarly, shoppers who are using coupons to take the sting out of their weekly food expenditures are frequently stocking up on items they'd otherwise pass by just because they're "getting a deal."

Value Assurance

Bargains are an assurance of value. Consumers often really don't know what things should cost. Sheena describes an experience common to many: "I saw a blue jersey wrap dress at Sears that was $49 on sale. I saw another at Talbot's that was $79 on sale. Then I see one at Bloomingdales that's nearly $300 and not on sale. Why? They seriously all look the same. The fabric feels the same. I feel like the one at Bloomingdales must be better in some way, like maybe if I waited and was able to get it at half price that I would be getting more for my money than the one that's $49 at Sears." When shoppers buy bargains, they feel more confident that they have been treated fairly and are therefore smarter about their purchases. Sales override the process of considering the value of an item. When consumers consider full-priced merchandise, they go through a price/value calculation. "Is it worth it? Is that a fair price?" When things go on sale, they are instinctively perceived as "a deal," and the lure of "savings" often overshadows the process of evaluating the product's worth. If that same product were at full price, shoppers would go through a more lengthy thought process to determine its value to them. Without this process, they're also more likely to make hasty, emotional purchases.

Competitive Sport Shopping

The thrill of the sale can feel like "winning" rather than spending. Sales create a sense of competition with other shoppers. Stacy, thirty-three, began getting emails from a favorite retailer about two-hour midday specials. "I had a few minutes during lunch and checked it out. They had La Mer moisturizer for half off! That never goes on sale. But it was sold out. So now I find myself rushing to check whenever I get the email, and I've noticed that most of the things on there get sold out right away. It's like a competition to see who can get it first." Getting the best deal or a great bargain is a badge of expertise for many shoppers, and the notion that they've won out over others through better planning, more effort, or expertise is rewarding to many consumers. The competition can overshadow a rational evaluation of the worth of the product in that person's life. Shoppers get the sense that they've "won" rather than "bought" an item.

Investing in the Purchase

The time, energy, and engagement required to sort through a jumble of markdowns or drive to an outlet mall is akin to an investment. Further, finding the right color, right size, or perfect brand is like unearthing buried treasure. Our perception of an item's value and our unconscious commitment to purchase gets a boost when we've already made a commitment of time. Our sense of good fortune when we find something good after a search rubs off onto the product and increases its emotional value. In other words, the hunt itself contributes to our perception of the value of the product. Diane says that she won't go to the luxury outlet mall located sixty miles from her home anymore. "It takes forever to get there. I think I must have figured if I drove all that way I couldn't leave empty-handed, so I've made some bad purchases over the years. Augh, even a $400 pair of boots that I couldn't return."

• • •

With all this psychological allure, discount culture is powerful. But the same emotional benefits can be offered to consumers—without the discounts. For example, clearly communicating the worth of a product is one way to give consumers the assurance of value that they need to purchase. Limited-edition or location-specific items activate the same "FOMO" feeling consumers get from sales. And offering logical reasons to buy (along with the more alluring emotional ones), such as a charity tie-in, provides shoppers with the rationalization they need to make a purchase.

These are all versions of the "plus one" that today's consumers are looking for when they shop—a bump in value, a boost in allure, or a bonus of some sort. Accustomed to bargains and overwhelmed with options, consumers must have a reason to buy now. In addition to the actual product they're buying, consumers expect something more, an incentive that will give them an extra emotional charge. Customization, an event, multiple uses for the product, entertaining pop-up stores, or a great story (such as a special product heritage or theme) are more examples of plus-one incentives that result in purchases. "Do-good" products such as those that tout being environmentally conscious or supporting communities offer not just one but three plus-one purchasing incentives: a compelling and human story, rationalization, and an emotional boost for the consumer who feels altruistic while spending. For example, consumers who purchase Tom's Shoes or Walgreen's flu shots are told that their purchase will result in a pair of shoes or a flu shot being donated to someone in need through each company's one-to-one matching program. Thus, in addition to their purchase, consumers also get to see themselves in a more positive light; they feel less wary about these businesses, which have been humanized through a compelling story of need; and they have the rationalization of giving rather than spending.

The Problem with Traditional Marketing Research

More emotionality and less rationality in purchasing decisions renders traditional marketing research, such as focus groups, less predictive. There's the problem that consumers often don't know how they feel. Even if they do, they may not be able to articulate those feelings. And even *then*, they might not want to share their feelings in front of strangers. Finally, consumers shop very differently when they're under the influence of elevated emotions: how someone feels when she's talking to a researcher isn't how she'll feel when she's shopping.

I'm often asked why consumers are unable to always behave in their best interests. People say they want healthy fast food, yet only 3 percent of visitors to McDonald's buy salads. They say they want to save money and then splurge. They're seen to be either morally or mentally weak.

But it's not so much weakness. Rather, we all frequently experience conflicting thoughts and feelings, especially when emotion intervenes during the decision process.

One way to envision this is that inside the mind of your customer is a committee. One member wants to save money, another is interested in quality, another just wants it to be a fast and easy decision, another is focused on avoiding guilt—and then there's the fun one who's willing to do what it takes to get an emotional kick. Each committee member is vying for control. The more sensible members of the committee speak for the group when we conduct marketing research that asks people to predict how they'll behave in the future. But in the purchasing moment, when emotions are in play, Mr. Fast and Easy, Ms. Fun, and occasionally Dr. Guilt have their way. When we're asked to evaluate products and anticipate what we'll do in the future, we tend to focus on product benefits and characteristics. But in the moment of purchase, we're more likely to shift our attention toward price and are more responsive to emotional cues.[28]

Retail Therapy

Despite, and even because of, the increased emotionality of consumers, many of them are looking for psychological or emotional relief through shopping. It works. A study conducted by TNS Global found that more than half of Americans admit to engaging in "retail therapy."[29] This echoes a previous study published in *Psychology & Marketing* which found that 62 percent of shoppers had purchased something to cheer themselves up, and another 28 percent had purchased as a form of celebration.[30]

Although "therapy" isn't quite the word I'd use to describe the positive effects of shopping, there are indeed psychological rewards. How else to explain the immense popularity of shopping? Here are five such rewards.

Easing Transitions

Janice had been in a marriage devoid of intimacy for over a decade. When she finally divorced, the first thing she did was to buy all new bedding. "It was like I was possessed. I spent hours shopping for just the right thing, and I finally bought the most beautiful duvet, shams, the works. It did feel therapeutic—like I was shedding that old marriage and ready to start fresh."

As part of a research project, I visited the home of Andre, a single thirty-nine-year-old tech entrepreneur, and was surprised to see he'd included a space for long dresses in his newly built custom closet. When I asked him about it, Andre said that he was "dating around" and hoped to get married soon. In, perhaps, an "If I build it, she will come" state of mind, Andre included what he thought were things his yet to be identified future wife would want. "I assume she'll need someplace to hang her dresses," he said.

Shopping can be a rich source of mental preparation. As people shop, they're naturally visualizing how they'll use the products they're considering, and in doing so they're also visualizing their new life. And as many athletes will attest, visualization is a performance booster and anxiety reducer.

It's no wonder then that two of the most shopping-intensive times of our lives are also two of life's greatest transitions: getting married and having a baby. The purchases themselves are only part of the allure; the preparation of shopping and visualizing makes people feel a greater sense of control and less anxiety about these big transitions. This also explains why sometimes the amount of shopping outweighs the actual needs.

Retail purchases can be helpful if the product inspires self-confidence and a sense of mastery. Whether we're shopping for dorm equipment with our teenager who is going off to college, or buying a special outfit to wear on vacation, and whether we're aware of it or not, nearly everyone has used shopping as a way to anticipate, imagine, and mentally prepare.

Dressing for Success

Annie admits that when she moved from her small rural hometown to Boston for a new job, she went overboard shopping for new clothes. "Everyone looked better than me; I had to get new stuff. I know I should be judged by just my work, but I really felt so much better when I'd come in with a great outfit. It's probably wrong that I wasn't confident without getting new clothes, but it was true, and it still is something I think is important."

What's unusual isn't that Annie purchased new clothing for her new job, city, and lifestyle but that she seemed to feel guilty about it. Who among us hasn't purchased something for a special date, a new job, or a big event? Turns out that buying and having the right outfit do affect our performance. In a study published by the *Journal of Experimental Social Psychology*, researchers had participants wear white coats and told them that they were doctors' coats. When wearing these coats, the participants were far more accurate on tests of attentional focus and concentration (traits associates with physicians) than the members of the control group, who simply wore their street clothes for the experiment.[31] On the flip side, we actually can judge a book by its cover—or, in this case, a person by his or her shoes. In a study published in the *Journal of Research in Personality*, participants were able to guess a person's age, gender, income, and agreeableness from photos of his or her shoes.[32]

The Pleasure Boost of Creativity and Aesthetics

Jules, a young administrative assistant, prides herself on her taste. "I love decorating and styling outfits. The texture and colors—I can think of just the right thing to tie it together. It's so fun." Jules enjoys shopping for creative inspiration. She says she visits shops at least once a week because "it's just fun to see what's new, and it gives me ideas."

Over the years, I've asked many consumers to describe products they love, and the responses have often struck me as similar to how someone might describe a piece of artwork. Marc, a fifty-six-year-old businessman, showed me a birthday gift from his wife, an expensive pen that he'd craved for years. He made sure I noticed every detail, including the smoothness of the case. He was clearly enraptured by the beauty and functionality of the pen. Some think that owning a luxury item is primarily about status, but for many the allure is craftsmanship and design that enlivens the senses.

Jules's shopping excursions serve a similar purpose. They enrich her life through creative expression and an appreciation of beauty and design. Judging by the monumental success of product pins on Pinterest, Jules isn't the only person inspired by the visual feast of retail.

Relaxation and Escape

When people think of the benefits of "retail therapy," mood elevation in the form of a temporary escape or the simple entertainment and rejuvenation of shopping are usually at the top of the list.

In my most recent consumer interviews, online shopping was increasingly mentioned as type of mini mental vacation, which makes sense. Unless purchasing is involved, it's a relatively mindless, relaxing activity.

Christina, a senior human relations professional, says that she shopped for light fixtures nearly every day for a couple of weeks during her lunch hour. "I'd just scroll and scroll. I kind of missed it when I finally bought one." Chanelle takes breaks from her family by shopping. "Sometimes it's crazy at home, so I go to the mall for some me time."

Be it window shopping, online scrolling, or pawing through racks at outlet malls, shopping really can be a mental refresher—like a blip of a vacation without any packing or planning. As a bonus, when we're faced with a difficult decision or arduous task, short breaks can actually improve performance and decision making. Studies show that our unconscious mind continues to work out problems while we're engaged in a different activity. (This shouldn't be confused with multitasking—doing several things at once—which results in not focusing on anything deeply.)

Social Connection

Since we first began gathering as humans, we've gone to the marketplace to connect with other people. "When I go on vacation, I always go to where people are shopping," says Elaine, a retired teacher. "I get a feel for the place and the people, especially if I'm traveling to a different country." Others, especially young people, meet friends and compare notes about tastes. "It's how I get to know someone," says Taylor, a stylish fifteen-year-old.

Some people feel connected with like-minded lovers of a particular brand. Elizabeth says, "I can spot an Alexander McQueen skull on a scarf, handbag, shoe, you name it, a mile away. Who spends that much money on a luxury item with a skull? Only people with a sense of humor. Like me."

If there's one antidote to emotional distress, it's human connection. We're a species that's meant to be with others of our kind; whether it occurs over dinner, at home, or at the mall, it's therapeutic.

Clearly there's a therapeutic role that shopping can play in the lives of consumers—and an equally clear need for a respite from the increasing stress, anxiety, and anger that we're all experiencing more frequently today. This represents an opportunity for the marketers who understand these emotional shifts to gain the love and loyalty of consumers—and a distinct competitive advantage.

The Consumer Call for Change

In the years that I've been interviewing consumers, there have always been love stories, there has always been finger-wagging, and consumers have always had lists of things that brands or retailers could do better. In the past year, however, I've noticed a change. Consumers are more vocal than ever. What they once might have appreciated, they now adore; what might have once irritated them now fully angers them; and their wish lists have grown. In short, consumers are more demanding, more emotional, and more vocal, and they want changes.

Today's consumers want to feel more in control; they want to feel seen and valued for more than their money; they're looking for brands and retailers that facilitate a sense of connection with others; and they want shopping and buying to be easier and more enjoyable. In Part Two, we'll discuss how to do all this. Each chapter outlines a recommended strategic adaptation to better satisfy today's new consumer psychology. It's fleshed out with tactics, cases, and examples that were either provided by or validated by the consumers I interviewed for this book.

Considering the sociocultural shifts we've discussed in the previous chapters, it's no wonder consumers want different things from retailers—they have a fundamentally different psychology.

Doug Stephens, author of *The Retail Revival*, sums up the need for change: "Virtually every aspect of life and society is up for debate right now. Privacy, human rights, marriage, gun control, health care, the environment, politics. You name it, *all* up for grabs. I can't ever remember a time when we as a society were actively rethinking so many paradigms and long-held beliefs. Yet I still see so many retailers simply retrenching their same old business models. Just doing what they've done for the last thirty years and trying to just be a little more competitive or efficient. In doing so, they're missing this unprecedented opportunity to completely reimagine, reshape, and reincarnate their businesses, and they may never get another opportunity like this to do so. Consumers, in my opinion, have never been more primed for change."[33]

Marketers have one of the hardest jobs in the world right now. They need to stay focused on an empathic, consumer-centric strategy while being smothered by tactical opportunities. They need to stay a step ahead despite today's incredible velocity of change. It's easy to miss what's important, the big essentials, when our daily lives are flooded with more details than ever. Yet doing nothing is not an option. Waiting is not an option. Today's consumer is not the same, so doing the same things won't work anymore.

PART TWO

Strategies to Connect with Today's New Consumer

4

Technovation

The strategies presented in these next chapters are the big essentials. They represent a shift in perspective on reaching consumers: impressing them with technology, reassuring them with a more authentic relationship, and involving them in a more intensified experience. Each strategy is augmented by tactics and examples for inspiration. There is no one-size-fits-all easy solution, and each brand and retailer will implement these strategies differently.

THE PATH TO PURCHASE IS PAVED WITH TECHNOLOGY

Digital technology is so integrated into the lives of consumers, it's like an additional body part—a third hand or a second brain. And just as consumers won't eat, sleep, work, or play without it, they're not shopping without it either. Everything about how and why consumers shop and buy has been affected by technology:

- As we talked about in Chapter One, technology has changed our practical, emotional, and relational needs. Those shifted needs have created new motivations for buying.
- People see, think, and make purchasing decisions with less attentional focus and more of an emphasis on visual cues.

- Consumers want to be able to use their computers, their smart-phones, and in-store technology to find the best prices, navigate offerings, learn about products, share with and learn from others, check inventory, and check out quickly.
- They want technology-enhanced smarter products and the thrill of wizardry in what they buy and how they shop.
- They want invitations to interact rather than intrusive message missives. And because they want what they want when they want it, and are increasingly frustrated by irrelevant marketing communications, they will use technology to filter, learn, share, and buy at the exact moment the mood strikes, be it online, in stores, or on the go.
- In addition to these wants, consumers view the retailers and brands that incorporate technology and innovation into their offerings as simply smarter, cooler, and more consumer-centric. Those that don't are thought of by many as simply not trying hard enough.
- Technology is also, increasingly, the medium that consumers are more comfortable using, favoring it over face-to-face interactions in retail environments.

All these factors demonstrate the importance of *technovation*—my hybrid word that means innovation with a technological edge. It is the new benchmark of excellence in retail and branding, and in this chapter we'll look at some ways successful marketers are doing it.

THE TECHNOVATION ADVANTAGE

Mood rings were ahead of their time. They were a hit in the 1970s and supposedly measured the wearer's emotions. Mood rings are actually liquid crystals bonded to quartz stones that change color according to temperature. Although they came with a little chart explaining what each color signified, a fever produced the same color as "frisky," and if you were outdoors in the winter without mittens, you were pretty much always "anxious" (and maybe you were if you'd lost your mittens!).

Today we have bracelets such as Jawbone Up and Fitbit Flex that keep track of our steps and sleep patterns, and they're every bit as big of a hit with consumers as mood rings were, but more accurate. Having the ability to know more about our bodies with the help of technology is increasingly the sort of innovation that consumers expect.

If fitness isn't your thing, there are also bracelets that multi-task as flash drives, computers, speaker phones, and televisions. Bracelets that can tell you when to reapply sunscreen or whether you've washed your hands long enough, or that help you keep track of your glucose level. And bracelets touted to relieve stress, fight bacteria, charge your cellphone with thermoelectric energy, detect poisonous gases, and generate solar power for later use as a night-light. There's also a bracelet that tells you when you're around someone you find attractive—if you need help figuring that out.

We're in love with technology. Companies that add a bit of science or technology to their offerings are thought of by consumers as smarter, trying harder, more interesting, and more relevant. Not every product lends itself to an added dose of technology, but every retailer and brand can up their impact through things like branded apps, advanced displays, superior website experiences, and tie-ins with more technologically oriented brands. As Lisa Parrish points out, "To adapt to the psyche of the American consumer, brands need to create more incredible, more technological shopping experiences."[1]

Consumers have a passionate sense of exploration, especially with technology. There's a fertile appetite for "new."
—John Digles[2]

For inspiration, here are a few examples of retailers that are using technovation to juice up the shopping experience.

Big Box Apps

The size and scope of offerings at Walmart is daunting to many consumers, especially when they're in a hurry. Same for IKEA, Home Depot, and Target. To the rescue are apps that help shoppers navigate stores and check inventories. Retailers can also add product codes to their merchandise so that consumers can see reviews, videos, or usage ideas.

Smartphone and Tablet Assistance

If you've visited an Apple store recently, you've probably noticed that it's "heads down" throughout the store. Apple has iPads next to each of their products, loaded with specifications, comparisons, and demos. This gives shoppers the opportunity to explore and learn on their own just as they'd do it at home—and as Alexis, herself a twenty-four-year-old sales associate, describes it, without "feeling the pressure of a salesperson breathing down your neck." As a bonus for those customers for whom eye contact is a less comfortable experience, when they do interact with a salesperson, they can do it side by side with their gaze directed toward the iPad rather than face-to-face.

Plants sold at Lowe's come with little plastic tags bearing codes that consumers can scan with their smartphones to get suggestions and videos about watering, planting, fertilizing, and optimal sunlight requirements.

Mobile Checkout

Retailers that have replaced cash registers with mobile checkout devices, such as Barney's, AT&T, and Anthropologie, help eliminate one of consumers' greatest sources of irritation: waiting. And the use of new technology elevates the stores in the minds of consumers.

Virtual Stores

Kate Spade used vacant storefront windows decked out with neon yellow, bold graphics, and . . . giant touch-screen displays to announce their new Saturday line of clothing and accessories. Purchases would be delivered anywhere in New York City in an hour. With a limited selection and a limited-time offering, these displays weren't designed primarily to drive immediate sales. They were much more. They got attention and demonstrated new, fresh-thinking brand values. In other venues, most notably South Korean train stations, virtual stores are grabbing a lot of consumer attention. They're giant LCD panels "stocked" with merchandise just like a store shelf. Shoppers order from their smartphones for delivery to their homes.

- Nearly three-quarters of shoppers would rather use their smartphones than consult store associates for simple tasks.[a]
- More than half of shoppers with smartphones believe that their using phones in stores will make shopping more fun.[b]
- Nearly half of smartphone owners have downloaded retailer apps.[c]
- Nearly 85 percent of smartphone owners used their phone to shop in the past month.[d]
- Nearly 50 percent of consumers believe they are more informed than store associates.[e]
- There are now more mobile connected devices on earth than there are people.[f]

BIG DATA AND TECHNOVATION

Decades ago, Chicago's Museum of Science and Industry learned that its baby chick hatchery was the museum's most popular exhibit by having observed excessive wear on the floor surrounding the hatchery. In response to this information, the museum enhanced the exhibit and created a better experience for museum goers.

Today, we learn what consumers love through "big data." From Google searches to retail transactions to GPS-enabled fitness monitors, we use over 2.5 *quintillion* bytes of data a day. Globally, consumers spend nearly $300,000 a minute shopping online and "like" more than 350,000 brands a minute on Facebook.[3] All of this information, and most particularly our social media behavior, hold clues to our feelings and beliefs: this is the ocean of data that analytic tools filter and interpret for retailers and brands to use in their approach to consumers.

The more a retailer knows about how a shopper behaves, the better they can serve that customer. Properly harvested, big data can assist nearly every stage of the marketing process and help to provide a truly customized and elevated shopping experience for consumers and stronger sales for marketers.

Techno-fueled, radically individualized consumers don't want to hunt through irrelevant merchandise or wade through ads that aren't all about them. They want the solutions that big data can provide. But retailers and brands must first show they can be trusted with consumer information, give customers a sense of control, and clearly demonstrate benefits of the trade-off.

Big data has very effectively been used, most notably by Amazon, to improve customer relationships and improve sales. It's used by online retailers to help their customers search more effectively and to encourage additional purchases. It's also an effective way to identify undersold offerings and opportunities and to measure the effectiveness of marketing communications and campaigns.

For example, big data is behind Netflix's sharpened effectiveness in helping their customers search through mountains of options. Netflix uses customer actions and an industry-praised algorithm to provide recommendations and a better real-time shopping experience. Netflix also uses big data to better understand how they should interact with their customers, testing new programs on sub-sets of their customers and comparing their actions against those of other groups.

Walmart developed its own search engine, Polaris, which they use on their website to better understand what someone is searching for in order to speed up and simplify the process. This uses another Walmart proprietary technology called the Social Genome, which "culls through millions of tweets, Facebook messages, blog postings and YouTube videos to detect purchase intent."[4]

Rent the Runway used an analysis of customer data to determine that a hefty percentage of their customers were adding accessories to their orders. Based on this information, they launched an upsell program. They also launched Our Runway, which features photos of their customers wearing their fashions. Users enter their height, bust, size, and age and then scroll through photos of similarly figured women wearing clothing they can rent. Women were 200 percent more likely to rent after seeing clothing on women shaped like them, compared to those who viewed the dress on a model.[5]

Online retailers have long had the ability to learn about how consumers shop by tracking their online movements and pur-chases. As a result, they've been able to provide recommendations, reviews, and services to expedite and inspire the shopping process. Shoppers consistently say they love these benefits, but many are also increasingly knowledgeable about—and wary of—how their personal information is being used. For example, brick-and-mortar stores that have attempted to replicate some of the processes used online by employing heat maps and tracking the Wi-Fi signals of shopper cellphones have faced some vigorous backlash.

Many consumers find behavior tracking and the collection of data related to their shopping behaviors to be an invasion of their privacy. The word I hear most often is "creepy." Generally speak-ing, younger consumers are significantly more willing to trade per-sonal information for convenience.

The wariness and backlash arise in part because we are all adjusting to more advanced forms of observation. And no matter how beneficial the personalized offerings, some consumers would simply rather have their privacy. But the crucial element retailers and brands need to pay attention to is *trust*. Retailers hoping to capitalize on big data will have to help customers understand aggregate data collection, offering benefits that outweigh the loss of privacy and earn their customers' trust.

Big data is a tool with big possibilities for marketers and consumers alike. It also has sharp elbows and a big head—that is, it has great potential to offend and disenfranchise creeped-out customers. Above all, regardless of the hype and of its real power, we have to remember that big data is simply a tool, not the ultimate solution to every problem. As Albert Einstein said, "Not everything that counts can be counted, and not everything that can be counted counts." Big data is not a replacement for creativity or the insights that come from experience. It's great at exploring how consumers are using what you have right now and testing ideas that have been already been generated. But it doesn't create the new ideas. So far, that's still a job for humans.

INTEGRATED SHOPPING: TEAR DOWN THOSE WALLS

People don't live their life online or offline—it's an increasingly integrated experience. Consumers are aching for a seamless, integrated shopping experience across all of the channels where they explore, research, purchase, and share. Nearly half of respondents in a recent Accenture survey believe that the best thing retailers can do to improve the shopping experience is to better integrate in-store, online, and mobile shopping channels. According to the study, "Regardless of their original shopping touchpoint—in-store, online or mobile—consumers expect their interaction with retailers to be a customized, uncomplicated and instantaneous experience."[6]

Ken Nisch, chairman of the retail design and strategy firm JGA, is one of the most influential people in retail design. According to Nisch, "There's a dance between mobile, Web, and bricks and mortar. It shouldn't be about who gets credit. Every experience is an opportunity. For example, the store's role in that dance is increasingly seen as pull marketing, that emotional connection that's more powerful than simply selling." Nisch uses the North Face, one of his clients, as an example. Customers can plan trips online, connect with athletes in-store, and receive offers on their mobile devices. Each medium reinforces the others. As Nisch says, "There's a dynamic, symbiotic connection between all three."[7]

During the nascent years of online shopping, retailers tried to comfort wary shoppers by creating an online environment that mimicked aspects of in-store shopping—like shopping carts. Today nearly 60 percent of consumers say their overall favorite way to shop is online.[8]

The opportunities today are in applying online successes to in-store environments and in better integrating every shopping experience, whatever the medium. For example, communities can be created online and in-store, each experience of community designed to reinforce the other. And both online and brick-and-mortar stores can simultaneously be places to buy as well as powerful brand-building communication tools. Most notably, consumers want a more technovated in-store shopping experience: they want all the benefits of online shopping brought into stores.

What shoppers tell me they like the most about online shopping:

- It's easy to find information and to research product characteristics.
- They get unbiased input from other purchasers through ratings and reviews.

(continued)

(continued)

- They can discover new products through site recommendations and "other shoppers bought" lists.
- They can compare prices across stores.
- They are assured of inventory.
- They can shop anywhere and at any time.
- It's fast—no driving, parking, or waiting in lines.

What shoppers tell me they like most about in-store shopping:

- They can see, touch, feel, and try on merchandise.
- It's easier to make a return.
- They can develop a relationship with a merchant.
- They can get their questions answered quickly and in real time.
- They enjoy browsing—it's more stimulating to the senses.
- It's a social activity.

Many retailers are scrambling to catch up to consumers in offering an integrated shopping experience. "Consumers move far more quickly than organizations," says Dave Hogue, former VP of user design at the digital agency Fluid.[9]

The challenge for most retailers is that they're organized into competing silos of expertise. Integrating the experience for consumers means reorganizing the business. Jason Goldberg is VP of strategy for the digital marketing firm Razorfish and on the board of directors of Shop.org, the digital division of the National Retail Federation. To his many fans and followers, he's known as "retail-geek." Goldberg has a three-part strategy to achieve the omnichannel integration consumers are craving.[10]

Set up new success criteria and new metrics. "You can't change siloed behaviors until you have new ways to measure happy success stories across channels. You have to give credit along the line rather than to only the point where the final transaction took place. That's how people interact with retailers; they're influenced across channels. Leaders are getting better about talking about the problems, but the metrics are still the same in most retail organizations. Divisions within companies are not only typically not aligned, but often they're in competition with each other—even adversarial because of this competition."

Designate an omnichannel leader. "With a VP of marketing, a VP of e-commerce, a VP of retail—who owns the customer experience? Companies that are restructured around a holistic consumer experience have greater integration and accountability. Macy's, for example, has a chief omnichannel officer, a very senior role with responsibility for an integrated customer experience."

Take an inventory of all the places your customer experiences your brand. "For many, that list will start with only a website, store, and call center. But your customer may also comment about their experience on Twitter, learn on Facebook, search on mobile, and so on. Customer journey mapping gives you the chance to figure out the good and bad of every aspect of the customer's experience with the brand. Invariably this becomes a horrifyingly long list."

Goldberg says that once the structure and process are in place, the answers will be specific to the retailer. But that structure and process will provide clarity, collaboration, and accountability. He adds that this new approach also encourages people to expand their expertise and move out of their comfort zones. "Most leaders grew up with one touchpoint as their main business. So their muscles around that one channel are typically more robust, and

also sometimes the least flexible. Changing legacy business practices and forming new habits is hard."

THE FUTURE OF BEAUTY

In the real world, what might the path a retailer takes from siloed
to integrated look like? Researchers at the world-renowned mas-
ter's in professional studies, cosmetics and fragrance marketing
and management program at New York's Fashion Institute of
Technology (FIT) think they might know. In addition to educating
the top executives in the beauty industry, the program is recognized
as the beauty industry's think tank. In 2013, the program's candi-
dates for graduation completed an extensive research project in
conjunction with Google on the future of beauty in a digital world.

Stephan Kanlian developed and chairs the program. According
to Kanlian, the beauty industry is currently overly dependent on
in-store transactions, with 95 percent of sales taking place in physical stores. Kanlian sees this as a challenge to the industry: "This is
due, in part, to the intimate nature of the products. But the industry is also underutilizing new opportunities in the digital realm."[11]

The research team believes that consumers want, even expect,
a more integrated shopping and buying experience, one that brings
technology into physical stores and a more human touch to online
and mobile shopping experiences. They also suggest, like Goldberg,
that operational and organizational changes will be necessary in
order to implement these shifts.

In-store predictions and recommendations for a more high-tech
experience involve leveraging artificial intelligence, facial recognition, and predictive analytics technology to personalize shopping,
and adding smaller, localized, and even pop-up stores in places like
airports and hotels that make shopping easier, more personal, and
more convenient.

The research team recommends adding a high-touch experience to online shopping by enabling consumers, via Xbox-type

technology, to virtually browse boutiques such as Chanel's flagship store in Paris or Sephora's flagship in Shanghai. Virtual beauty advisers would be available to answer questions as shoppers browse, and purchases can be made online.

L'Oreal, one of the industry partners to the FIT program, already has an Xbox app, the Next Level, which is touted to be a "one stop beauty and style hub for women where they can watch how-to videos and gain more information on products."[12] With an "engage" rather than "interrupt" philosophy, the app is intended to be an entertaining style and fashion experience.

The team envisions "beauty on demand" as the future of their industry. Kanlian described it as "the street becoming the mall." Using Google visual image recognition and color matching technology, shoppers would be able to do things like snap a photo and search for that color of lipstick, purchase from a shop window at midnight from their phone, or order what an actress is wearing on TV.

Kanlian, the research team, and their advisory board, which is made up of senior executives from every major beauty company, believe the future of beauty is in using ROL (return on learning) rather than simply ROI (return on investment) as the new metric to track and drive brand value.

• • •

The use of technology has radically changed the psychology of consumers and created a crop of new needs and expectations. Ironically, some of those needs are also partially met by incorporating technology and innovation into brands, products, and the retail environment. The consumer-centric use of big data to facilitate fast, personalized, easier shopping; brand and retail experiences that integrate online and digital realms; and the allure and assurance of technology-infused products are the solutions today's consumers demand.

5

The Real Deal

Today's consumers are defensive and distrustful. They're disengaging from relationships with brands because those relationships lack the foundational ingredient of trust. Previous generations of marketers had it easier: their job was to maintain a trust that was assumed. For all the reasons covered in Part One of this book, today the consumer fallback position is distrust. Today, marketers are working from a deficit.

"They're just trying to sell me things" is what I typically hear from consumers who are concerned about retailer tactics. The implication is that retailers are employing trickery or manipulation that tilts the scales away from a fair and equitable exchange of money for wanted products. It's a protective mentality borne of distrust.

Consumers *want* to trust. They want the faster, simpler, and more enjoyable transactions made possible by trust. They want the sense of belonging that comes with loyalty. Yes, they are dazzled by "new" and are more eager than ever to explore new options. And yes, they also love to champion new retailers and brands to tout their own shopping expertise. But they also want the comfort, simplicity, and pleasure of doing business with brands and retailers they know and trust. And they can get it all—both familiarity and the thrill of new—when retailers and brands build trust through humanity, personality, and authenticity delivered with a dose of technovation.

There's another reason why authenticity and the real deal are so potent today—they're the antidote to our online lives. As more and more of our time is spent in a photoshopped, intangible, and virtual online world, we increasingly crave what feels real and genuine.

USING PSYCHOLOGY TO BUILD CONSUMER TRUST

Obviously, the foundation of a more authentic brand experience is trust. That starts with promising only what you can deliver and delivering on your promises. Most brands and retailers do just that. Today it takes more. A brand that feels solid, authentic, and real is one that

- Cares and has the courage and confidence to listen without defensiveness
- Is sincere in showing its need and appreciation for its customers
- Is so clear about its integrity that it shares openly and unashamedly
- Has a distinct personality, anthem, and community

- The fifty brands showing the fastest financial growth from 2000 to 2010 were all associated with one of five positive human traits: eliciting joy, enabling connection, inspiring exploration, evoking pride, or impacting society.[a]
- According to Young & Rubicam's Brand Asset Valuator, in recent years the brand value "Kindness and Empathy" has increased in importance to consumers by 391 percent, and "Friendly" is up 148 percent.[b]

In interpersonal relationships, shame is a barrier to connection. It creates murky communications, inauthenticity, and defensiveness. *Shame is what consumers infer when brands aren't "real."* They wonder what retailers and brands are hiding. Starting with integrity, and having and showing confidence that you're delivering value, are at the core of your consumer's trust. For example, to address the perception that they were misleading customers in their advertising, McDonald's created YouTube videos that confidently explain why the products consumers buy look different than the ones in McDonald's ads.

Beyond the authenticity that establishes trust, genuine, real brands are created through

- The rub-off: experiences such as YouTube videos or events that create emotions that "rub off" onto brands
- Humanizing: using the potential of social media and championing employees and customers to create a more personified brand
- Consistency: brand characteristics and values that are so consistently communicated with language that's so genuine that they're actually heard
- Anchoring: brand stories made more relatable and genuine by their association with familiar images, places, times, experiences, or things

Let's see how each of these works.

The Rub-Off

"Extreme Sheep LED Art" is the title of a YouTube video that's been viewed nearly nineteen million times. It's the most impressive display of sheep herding imaginable. The sheep wear LED-lit vests, and the action takes place at night. Among other things, the sheep are herded to simulate a Pong game and create a fireworks display.

The video has a homemade quality, and it isn't until the very end that you see that it's sponsored by Samsung.

Only the most jaded soul could watch this video without feeling at least a touch of excitement and awe. And it's in that frame of mind that you see the Samsung logo. Because our minds don't perfectly connect the stimulus to our emotional response, we are left feeling awed and excited by Samsung, even if we're not consciously aware of it.

If that's a tough idea to swallow, let me offer more proof. There are numerous psychological studies that demonstrate this effect; this one is a classic. Researchers had male participants walk across a narrow suspension bridge above a deep ravine. They were met at the other end by a female researcher who asked them a few questions. Another group was instructed to walk across a more stable bridge. Those who walked across the scary bridge, and therefore had an elevated heart rate because of a touch of fear, were more attracted to the researcher than the safe-bridge group. They unconsciously attributed their elevated heart rate to sexual arousal, when really it was due to the fear of falling. The participants attached their response to the wrong stimulus.[1]

This sort of mental leap, or blurring, is what Samsung is using with "Extreme Sheep." And in turn, "Extreme Sheep" is part of the reason why Samsung is the laptop and cellphone manufacturer with the highest rating for emotional engagement.[2]

Red Bull has also mastered this technique by sponsoring extreme events such as Fearless Felix's 840-mph stratospheric free fall, during which Red Bull's distinctive logo was visible from every angle. The thrill of the event infuses people's feelings about the brand.

So when people have fun at retailer parties, when they're moved by a brand's charitable efforts, or when they're thrilled at sporting events, those positive emotions do more than engage consumers; they actually become the essence of a brand and are more real and moving than anything a brand can say about itself.

Humanizing

Here's how Julie Zischke, a twenty-four-year-old manager in New York, describes her evolving "relationship" with the Rebecca Minkoff brand:

> I became a fan of Rebecca Minkoff the company, the person, before I became a fan of Rebecca Minkoff, the product. She established such a strong social media presence that I actually felt a connection to her almost more comparable to a blogger than to a brand. I've been a fan of hers for almost three years, I would say, but I didn't buy my first Rebecca Minkoff bag until December of last year. My connection with the brand, though, is strong enough that I feel proud that I own it. It's a very popular brand now, and it seems everyone has the same purse of hers, but I like her despite this, not because of it. I guess I have a sense of ownership or investment in the company, like I got to see some of it happen. I admire her for representing herself in a very true and real way; you get to feel like you know her.[3]

Consumers view the directness and intimacy of social media as access to a brand's soul. That access provides the insight they need to understand the personality and values of a brand—its human characteristics. The way you use social media depends of course on the personality of your brand.

Facebook community or website forums that facilitate discussion about retailers, products, or brand values offer the kind of access, insight, and sense of partnership that consumers crave. Kraft's online community forum gets hundreds of comments about more than what to do with cheese. People share weight loss problems and party ideas, and ask "Kraft Kitchen" personnel to dig up recipes their mom made.

Similarly, brands that showcase their customers on their web-sites or Facebook pages add a relatable and real component to the brand. Many brands, such as Tiffany, ask for photos from their cus-tomers, pick the best, and post them on their websites. Others, such as Lululemon, encourage their customers to upload photos themselves via Instagram. Lululemon generated more than two million page views and a million Instagram "likes" when they issued a call for their customers to post photos of themselves under the hashtag #thesweatlife.[4] Besides the involvement this generates, everyday people as models are more relatable and real than profes-sional models.

Directly replying to Twitter comments and customer service issues goes miles toward humanizing a brand. When Kathy tweeted that she loved the soup being served in the Air Canada lounge, she got a reply within minutes. She said that their reply, "Glad you like the soup, Kathy," was both unexpected and heartwarming to her. More than half of consumers believe that companies are more responsive to consumers when they complain via social media. There are high expectations, though: nearly half also say that it annoys them when they don't get a fast response from a company they contact via social media.[5]

Applying human characteristics to products—tapping into that instinct we all have to anthropomorphize—isn't new, but it works better than ever because of our technology-induced connection deficits. "Baby" carrots are more lovable. They're also tremendously handy, but calling them "baby" has helped consumers trust and try them. "Skinny" has been equally effective as a more human, humorous, and benefit-oriented way to shout "diet." Skinny Girl cocktails, Skinny Pop popcorn, and Skinny Cow frozen desserts are chic, approachable, and humanized through their association with the "it" word "skinny." In the case of "skinny," there is also a dose of immediate gratification through an identification with the benefit. Contrast that with Diet Margarita. Sounds awful, right? There's nothing fun, social, or human about Diet Margarita. It's all sacrifice, no benefit.

More than 80 percent of Internet retailers respond to customer service performance issues on Twitter. The average
response time is nearly twelve hours.[c]

Nothing speaks louder than the voices of a brand's employees.
A golf store sharing Vine or Instagram videos of great courses,
swings, or putts from their customers and employees demonstrates
a passion for the sport beyond selling products.

Authenticity is the new black.

—Jason Dubroy[7]

More than three-quarters of consumers think of the voices
of employees—through website and Facebook blogs, videos, and
stories—as evidence that a company is interested in building a good
relationship. And nearly seven in ten consumers say they spend time
reading content from a brand of interest.[6] Interviews with staff members, customer success stories, how-to contests, and, of course, visuals
are a few of the types of content that consumers tell me they love.

One Kings Lane's use of visual communication coupled with the
clear and distinct personality of the site establish the trust necessary
to get shoppers to snap up unbranded, four thousand dollar, non-
returnable sofas that they haven't seen in person. One Kings Lane
sells luxury home furnishings ranging from coffee mugs to rugs and
furnishings running well into the thousands. They do it flash sale
style, only online, and most of their products can't be returned or
exchanged. In fewer than five years the retailer has gained more than
eight million members, 85,000 Facebook "likes," and they have pro-
jected annual revenues of more than $300 million. That's especially
impressive because consumers are particularly hesitant to make four
kinds of purchases: things they'll keep for a long time, expensive
things, things that they can't return, and things they're not familiar

with or can't see and touch—like many of the products One Kings Lane sells out of every day. How? This could only have been accomplished through trust. The authentic, tasteful visuals of the site coupled with the implicit endorsement of the top decorators and designers who participate in curated special offerings create a sense of intimacy and authority that's similar to old-school book, wine, and record store employee recommendations.

In another take on featuring employees to represent and humanize a brand, AAA highlights warm, approachable-looking employees on attention-getting yellow billboards in Northern California. Each employee has "superhero expertise" in his or her work at AAA, such as "masterful tire changer," "fabulous cruise planner," or "DMV paperwork whiz." Each employee also has a quirky, relatable personality "flaw" such as "so-so softball player" or "sewing challenged."

These billboards hit the psychological jackpot. First, they tap into a strong color association with AAA's rescue vehicles. Considering AAA's massive membership base, a healthy percentage of drivers probably unconsciously associate that shade of yellow with the relief and gratitude they felt when they received a AAA jump-start or tow in the past. That's an excellent mind frame to be in when processing new AAA messages. Second, a company that champions their employees—praising their professional skills and demonstrating personal knowledge of them—appears more trustworthy and genuine. It's a subtle, humble, and credible way to advertise AAA offerings, and one that works especially well for AAA because their employees *are* their product. Last, the employees' flaws make all of this possible. Mentioning them humanizes the employees, which humanizes the brand. They allow a brag to be acceptable and are interesting enough to capture attention. As an added benefit, ads like these boost employee pride, which can lead to improved performance and advocacy.

Billtrust, an outsourced billing solutions company, executed a similar business-to-business campaign. They created a "Billing

Rockstar" award to recognize excellence in the billing profession, what Billtrust CEO Flint Lane admits is "not the sexiest part of an organization." After a nomination and voting process, winners receive a platinum album award. Drew Neisser, CEO of Renegade, a social media and marketing agency and a popular blogger for *Fast Company*, says the program has been successful because "by shining a light on successful billing professionals, Billtrust has generated tremendous goodwill from its customers, who appreciate the recognition and who in turn provide powerful testimonials about the efficacy of Billtrust solutions."[8] Recently, Billtrust created ads featuring two of their Billing Rockstars. "What started out as a customer engagement plan has now come full circle, continuing to celebrate client success but now being used to also attract new customers," says Neisser.

And then, of course, there is the in-person humanizing experience. Chris's encounter with a "bunny bowl" forever changed her perception of a trendy Los Angeles restaurant. "I asked for extra sauce, and they brought it in a little ceramic bowl shaped like a bunny. It was so charming and sweet. I asked where they'd purchased it, and the waiter said it was the chef's own property, that he loved to collect vintage ceramic serving dishes. It was so unexpected and so personal. I love that restaurant ten times more now."

Whether they do so consciously or not, consumers *will* attribute a personality to your brand in their quest for a shorthand, emotional understanding of your brand's values. The people who represent your brand are part of that perception. Every visual, olfactory, auditory, and symbolic attribute also contributes—including a brand's policies on customer engagement.

> Nearly 80 percent of Americans say that their relationship with brands is much more personal than ever before.[d]

Consistency and the Word on Words

Every experience contributes to consumers' perception of your brand. Ever vigilant, they're on the lookout for mismatches, which can make them feel manipulated, disrespected, or lied to. And no matter how good you are at implementing a "visual over verbal" strategy, eventually you'll need to use words. The love and human connection a retailer or brand has earned through authenticity can fall apart in the fine print.

Consumers frequently point to "legalese" and "corporate speak" as evidence that brands and retailers are not to be trusted. Here are a few of the many stories shoppers have shared with me:

> I had a horrible flashback when my new coffee-maker arrived. The instructions were so complicated. Remember when everything came with a big manual of "do this" and "fear that"? This company is evidently still in the dark ages.

> Why do companies say "to serve you better" when they want you to do something? I don't see them serving me better. I see them bullshitting me.

> Whenever I hear clichés like "buy now" or "for a limited time only," I think of those Ginsu knives they used to sell on late-night TV.

> I was all set to buy some wonderful shoes during an online promotion where everything was supposed to be 20 percent off. But then there is this long, I mean *long*, list of brands that were excluded, and of course the shoes I wanted were on there. It just really turned me off; I felt tricked.

In an exercise where I've asked shoppers to help me understand what's influenced them to make—or skip—a purchase, a few principles have surfaced around the use of language:

- Don't let your lawyers write your copy. If they must get their say, humanize their passage with an introduction.
- Ban clichés. We're exposed to the same words and phrases over and over in our professions. Just as we bristle when we hear "cutting-edge" or "outside the box" or "keep calm and [insert personal touch here]," consumers bristle when they hear "once in a lifetime opportunity," "state-of-the-art," or "you deserve." Whatever you're trying to say, you can say it better, and more honestly, than that.
- Refresh language as often as possible. Consumers become habituated to language and content quickly. When this happens, they don't see it. Or worse yet, they become irritated. Very subtle changes, especially in advertisements, can refresh your customer's interest. For example, in an experiment where participants were exposed to multiple viewings of a print advertisement, a group who saw variations on the ad where the logo had been moved were 19 percent more likely to choose that product than a group who saw only the same ad over and over.[9]
- Stay positive. For today's anxious consumers, positive language works better and feels more caring. "There's still time, final hours" works better than "Only two hours left—don't miss out." Similarly, accentuating the positive (you get this good thing) instead of the negative (you won't get that bad thing) falls on more receptive ears. For example, "clear skin" beats "no more pimples"—and, as we saw earlier, "skinny" beats "diet" by a mile.

Anchoring

There is another discipline that strong brands and retailers use to establish a sense of authenticity: anchoring. Great brands have a story—often one that's still unfolding. Through that story, they're anchored in something that goes beyond having a product to sell—something richer, more meaningful and human. And they often keep that story alive with new chapters and constant engagement.

For example, what do Cowgirl Creamery, Coors, and Campbell's have in common besides the letter C?

Each evokes a place, an image, or a time. The Cowgirl Creamery brand name alone says it all, though of course the company goes well beyond relying on a name. Every aspect of their brand, from the chalkboard signs to their pared-down packaging, is anchored in an image and a story. Coors has long capitalized on their Colorado Rockies heritage, in packaging, advertisements, and expressions of the brand's value proposition. And Campbell's? They've managed to update their products to meet new consumer needs and tastes, but the brand is firmly planted in a trustworthy history that exists in the childhood memories of a legion of Baby Boomers.

Sometimes brands borrow the story anchors of other products, often for temporary use. For example, old tackle boxes, typewriters, and sewing machines are popping up in displays at dozens of contemporary stores. The heritage, longevity, and history of these products evoke a sense of security and permanence that elevates the quality of the products in the store. Similarly, when J. Crew explains the history of a *type* of sweater they're selling (going back as far as sixteenth-century Scotland) and talks about the iconic men associated with that sweater (such as Steve McQueen and the Duke of Windsor), they leverage some of that sweater's heritage to create a longer, deeper story of their own.

A BRAND THAT DOES IT ALL

Panerai, the Italian-born watch company that is now a subsidiary of the Richemont Group, has created an effective model for differentiating its brand in a crowded, high-margin market, by focusing on three strategies that drive engagement with consumers: authenticity, scarcity, and community. The brand has stayed true to its own personality and its story even as it has introduced innovations, and consumers have rewarded it with trust, admiration, and enthusiasm.

Authenticity

As a consumer brand, Panerai is relatively new. It wasn't until the mid-1990s that the brand made a serious push into the consumer market. But by that time, the company was already more than 130 years old. It came with a rich history dating back to 1860, when Giovanni Panerai began a small, family-owned business making high-quality pocket watches. Giovanni may have been content with the scope of his business, but his son Guido had bigger ambitions and moved the company into production of high-precision instruments for the Royal Italian Navy.

Guido envisioned a bright future—literally. Around 1910, he began experimenting with a mixture of zinc sulphide and radium bromide to enable his watches to glow in the dark, particularly important for Italian navy divers. He called the substance Radiomir, which became the name for Panerai's first and celebrated wristwatch model.

Panerai continued a string of innovations, including extra-large cases to aid legibility underwater; screw-down crowns and half-moon clasps that guarded crowns; rugged straps; titanium cases; and a new luminous substance made with tritium that the company branded Luminor (which became the name of another famous watch model). In 1993, Panerai created a numbered series in limited editions of models aimed at the consumer market. When Sylvester Stallone wore one of their watches in the movie *Daylight* in 1995, consumer demand began to grow, and in 1997, a Richemont predecessor company, Vendome Group, bought the company and launched the brand to the global consumer market.

Today, Panerai's marketing heavily leverages this rich historical legacy of the company. Many of its watch styles remain true to original designs, imparting a patina of history, pedigree, and substance. In one of its newest models, introduced in 2012, the company icon of two divers from the Royal Italian Navy riding a small submarine (what Panerai aficionados call the "pig") is very subtly embossed on the face. In an age of pop-up stores and other consumer ephemera, the legacy of Panerai speaks to the desire we all have for depth, meaning, and authenticity.

Scarcity

When Panerai started producing for the consumer market in 1993, it began with limited editions of its products and continues with that strategy today. Basic model platforms don't change, but each year versions are introduced with new features, and historical models that have been shelved for decades are sometimes refreshed and revived. These are not mass-market watches, although demand for them has continually risen over the past twenty years. They are released in limited quantities, ranging from 250 to 2,000 depending on the model. The company generally unveils new models early in the year, but delays actual release until later in the year, allowing Panerai enthusiasts to build up a lot of chatter in the meantime. This chatter effectively drives up anticipation of the new watches' arrival, and when they finally do reach the market, many people buy quickly for fear of missing out, especially on limited runs. Typically, a few models each year become investment watches, with original prices being driven up by demand and scarcity. It will be an ongoing challenge for Richemont to sustain the balance of scarcity and demand, but so far they seem to have figured it out.

Community

Probably due to a combination of history and scarcity, Panerai has developed a large and passionate community of buyers and collectors. Since 2000, Paneristi.com has served as a gathering site for the brand's devotees. On a typical day, literally hundreds of Panerai owners and aspirants post photos, comments, anecdotes, experiences, and advice on all things Panerai. Post that it's your birthday, and you'll be swarmed with good wishes. Ask somebody, "What are you wearing today?" and within a few hours there are dozens of wrist shots.

"I put together a post of some of my favorite things—things that represent perfection, including my small Panerai collection— and within a few hours people were gushing over it," said Bob, a middle-aged business executive. "I actually felt an emotional connection with these people, and it seemed to give more meaning and resonance to my watches. It feels like a true community."

Bob's Panerai community took on physical dimensions when he was invited to a Panerai "GTG," or get-together, in San Francisco. It was hosted by a local dealer showing off new models, and drew about 150 Panerai fans who spent the evening with conversation and cocktails. "I knew no one when I went in the room and came out with several new friends," said Bob. "It also brought me closer to the brand."

Of course, much of the Panerai community grew organically from the ground up. If you spend $8,000 on a watch (close to the average price of a Panerai), you're likely to feel passionate about it. But Panerai was very astute about this phenomenon, and in 2010 took a step that galvanized the Panerai community. Partly to celebrate the tenth anniversary of Paneristi.com and the rise of the community, the company solicited input from customers on what the perfect Panerai model would look like. The result was the PAM 360 model, known affectionately as the "BBQ" model in honor of a Paneristi.com forum member who had passed away and had the screen name WWBBQD. Only three hundred of this model were manufactured. It was not sold at retail, but given away through a lottery. With one product, Panerai managed to incorporate crowdsourcing, scarcity, customer loyalty, and authenticity in a powerful act of brand building.

• • •

I haven't found that consumers are consciously aware of how much they crave things that are real, brands that feel authentic, and relationships they can trust. But this need becomes a clear and resounding theme when I interview consumers about exceptional interactions, purchases, and brands. Honesty, authenticity, consistency and dependability, humanity, and genuine emotions—these are the virtues of the real deal. They're the refreshing and memorable antidote to our overstimulated, semi-virtual, sound-bite lives.

6

Involvement

In olden times (say, ten years ago) a company would make a great product, set a tempting price, tell the people most likely to be interested all about it, and sell the product. It was so simple back then. Control over nearly every aspect of the transaction was in the hands of the company—except for the decision to buy. Consumers sat back and let the experts do the driving. If the offer came together in a way that pleased them, they purchased.

Today, people are willing to be involved in every aspect of that process—from what's made, to how it's produced, to where it's sold. They are willing to engage in promoting and even selling it themselves. Many even insist on this level of involvement.

NEW-SCHOOL MARKETING

This shift is occurring partly because it's possible today and wasn't ten years ago. But more important, it is occurring because consumers are more individualistic and want uniqueness and the opportunity to be recognized; further, it has to do with their diminished trust that others will care for them or give them what they need—they're used to being more self-reliant. The fact that consumers are willing to devote their time and energy to marketing activities is a testament to the importance of products and retail in their lives.

A more involved customer is great news for the marketers who have adjusted to this change. Obviously it's an enormous lift to be ready to harvest feedback for design, facilitate social media engagement, reward champions, or host contests. Not every tactic in this chapter is the right fit for every company, but every business has an opportunity to involve their customers. And when they do so, genuinely and responsively, they build trust, excitement, and loyalty—and better products and services.

Today's consumers come to know you and love you through how you engage, interact, and respond, what you do, and how you present yourself. Words are less relevant; the consumer is in effect saying, "Put your money where your mouth is." Another way of saying this is that old-school marketing championed the brand, whereas new-school marketing champions the consumer—who then champions the brand.

Very Old School
1. You want people to try your new tissues.
2. You purchase a targeted list.
3. You mail consumers an unrequested box of tissues.
4. They're happy to get the tissues.

Old School
1. You want people to try your new tissues.
2. You purchase media asking consumers to visit your website or Facebook page to request a free sample.
3. You mail them the requested box of tissues.
4. They're happy and feel smart for getting free tissues.

New School
1. You want people to try your new tissues.
2. During cold and flu season, you launch an advertising campaign and set loose your social media team.

3. You offer consumers the opportunity to visit your website so that they can send a free box of tissues to their sniffling and sneezing friends as a gesture of caring.
4. You round things out by offering to send virtual tissues from your Facebook page.
5. Bloggers go wild. Publicity is immense. Word-of-mouth is glowing.
6. You send out millions of samples—over forty-five thousand on your busiest day.
7. You're magnanimous in the eyes of consumers. The senders are happy, the recipients are happy, and goodwill toward your brand flourishes. The tissues seem even softer because of all those positive feelings.
8. After two years of declining revenue and market share, you bounce back because of this campaign.

Kleenex's "Share the Softness" campaign, described here, is new-school marketing at its finest. It highlights the benefits of serving rather than selling and the power of emotionally invigorating your customers.

THE FOUR C'S OF INVOLVEMENT

I've found four major opportunities to involve your customer at various points in your product's life cycle. Handily, each begins with the letter C. They are

- Champions
- Customization
- Crowdsourcing
- Contests

The best type of involvement is whatever is the most natural extension of your brand or product, and it requires creativity and effort—but it's worth it. These C's turn passive consumers into your advocates, your allies, and potentially your most satisfied, trusting, and committed customers.

Champions

Brands and retailers are no longer defined exclusively by what they have to say about themselves. Today consumers are more interested in what other consumers, employees, bloggers, and the media have to say. Consumers who are willing to vouch for, recommend, or discuss your brand not only help spread the word but also are more credible. Imagine someone walking into a cocktail party yelling, "I'm here and I'm great! Check me out!" We've all known people like that, and they're just not that popular. The same is true for modern branding. It's much more effective to inspire others to do the talking—to cultivate champions for your brand.

Social media is the tool of champions. The fundamentals are the ratings and reviews of users on brand websites and review websites such as Yelp and Angie's List. Beyond those basics, marketers have an array of other opportunities to beckon the engagement of consumers who will champion their brand.

Bloggers

Whether they're responsible for the runaway success of a $10 robotic hamster toy or the birth of successful makeup lines, bloggers clearly influence consumers. Whether they post on a YouTube channel or a website, they spread the word of mouth that consumers trust.

Sales of my first book, *Gen BuY*, took a mighty jump the day that Generation Y expert Dan Schwabel posted an interview with me on his popular blog. People trust Dan.

To connect with bloggers, marketers need to intrigue them. Most are looking for content. Therefore, your own blogs, social media content, contests, and direct outreach can be as important to them as they can be to you. The robotic hamster got a boost from influential "mommy bloggers" who were sent hamster party kits that included games, snacks, and, of course, Mr. Squiggles and Num Nums, the hamster toys. Zhu Zhu Pet Hamsters became one of the first examples of the power of bloggers to champion brands. Due in part to the credible words of bloggers, Zhu Zhu hamsters became *the* hot holiday toy of 2009—selling for triple their retail price on Amazon and eBay.

According to a survey of seven hundred mothers, 90 percent believe that social media has empowered them, 78 percent believe that social media gives brands a more personal touch that helps generate loyalty, and 55 percent have tweeted a brand about a customer service issue.[a]

Social media has the power to turn an individual into an information or advertising medium. You can think of bloggers as a kind of celebrity: they have less allure, but they're more credible. Think of the difference between a movie star and a makeup artist to the stars who demonstrates techniques on YouTube. The star can certainly create an image and exposure; the makeup artist has a different but equally powerful kind of allure: credibility.

Facebook

More than 60 percent of online consumers follow or give feedback to brands on social media sites.[1] A few highly likable brands, such as Amazon, Coke, and Disney, get the majority of their "thumbs-ups" as a show of support and genuine liking. Of Coke's seventy million Facebook fans, more people than not have "liked" them because they just plain like them.

The more typical brand is getting "liked" because their consumer has been incentivized. They "like" in exchange for a coupon, a discount, or insider knowledge of upcoming sales. Although not the optimal kind of brand love, those "likes" matter anyway. Consumers wouldn't want your discounts if they didn't like you—so there is some genuine love, or at least liking, there. And new customers are swayed by the wisdom of the crowd. They assume that a highly liked brand or retailer must be good.

> Less than 20 percent of small business websites have a link to a Facebook page, and even fewer have links to Twitter and LinkedIn.[b]

Juicy visuals, contests, witty questions, intriguing stories, and engagement campaigns such as the tissue giveaway create a more intimate Facebook courtship. Facebook as a component of larger campaigns and contests is becoming de rigueur.

Twitter

Can you engage with 140 characters? Indeed you can. Followers are, again, interested in discounts, but many simply enjoy knowing more about brands. Twitter is also a popular customer service vehicle. Monitoring and quickly addressing complaints (and compliments) about your brand on Twitter is impressive to consumers.

Generous engagement and recognition of follower comments are emotionally potent. Humor, humanity, and an authentic voice are essential. But most important is sharable content that highlights your authority in your field. Hat's off to the *New Yorker* for its highly engaging Twitter feed; the content has personality, and, most important, it's highly sharable. It's no wonder they have 2.5 million followers.

> More than one-quarter of the time that Americans spend online is devoted to social media sites.[c] Nearly 45 percent of Americans say that social networking keeps them in the know about brands and products. That number rises to 63 percent for the thirty-five-and-under demographic.[d]

Pinterest

The visual feast of Pinterest is just the sort of fast, emotional connection that inspires the wanting, needing, and loving mentioned earlier in this book. In a recent qualitative survey, I asked young adults, "How do you usually find out about new things you might like to buy?" More than half of the women I surveyed mentioned Pinterest. Unsurprisingly, none of the men mentioned Pinterest in any part of the survey, which matches the profile of Pinterest's users. Nearly 97 percent of Pinterest's Facebook fans are women,[2] and more than 70 percent of its users are women.[3]

Within ten months of its March 2010 launch, Pinterest had seventy million users. Obviously Pinterest hit a chord—particularly with women. Nordstrom has more than 4.5 million followers on Pinterest. The retailer facilitates drill-down interest with targeted boards for lovers of things like "arm candy" and "shiny things." Scrolling through Nordstrom's Pinterest site is shopping in disguise. Nordstrom also uses Pinterest to technovate in-store by placing Pinterest "P" logos next to the most pinned products.

General Electric pins interesting facts, educational games, infographics, and factory photos on their site. Without saying a word, they communicate a devotion to science and technology that elevates their brand. To fast-track an emotional connection with consumers, create a delightful and inspiring visual representation of the values of your brand.

Content is judged on its ability to be shared. It can't just be excellent; it has to be sharable.

—Jason Dubroy[4]

Video

Fast, easy, and emotionally rich, video engages our senses, which makes it an especially effective way to connect with today's customers. More than 85 percent of online adults watch videos each month hoping to be informed, educated, and entertained.[5] There is still an audience for YouTube kitty videos, but consumers have been increasingly turning to brand-sponsored videos for some of the finest content on YouTube.

Lowe's how-to videos have been viewed by millions on YouTube. Among other things, viewers can learn how to remove wallpaper in thirty seconds or how to install a new faucet in five minutes. Social media pros that they are, Lowe's also answers home and garden questions like "How do I get rid of moss?" on Twitter. Lowe's doesn't miss an opportunity to position themselves as home and garden experts. Their help is appreciated, their authority is established, and through their smart, committed engagement with social media, they win an emotional rapport with consumers.

Vine and Instagram video snippets bring tweets and posts to life, which enhances engagement. For example, Lululemon gets seven times as many comments on their Instagram videos as they do on their photos, and General Electric gets five times their usual level of engagement by posting videos on Facebook.[6]

In a society that increasingly values "watching," video presents an opportunity for creative marketers. Honda responds to tweets with the hashtag #wantnewcar with personalized six-second Vine performances, which are later incorporated into TV spots and online ads. The first day of the campaign resulted in more than twenty-two hundred Twitter mentions.[7]

• • •

Social media works brilliantly for the big guys, but it is a powerful tool for smaller, start-up, and niche brands too. Greg Berardi runs a public relations and social media firm for entrepreneurial companies. He says, "Social is marketing, and it is the new word-of-mouth. It's actually better than that. A person with a thoughtful social presence can reach many, many more people than they ever could being on the cocktail party circuit. A strong social presence will generate leads over time if that is your goal, or make you more influential if changing the world is your mission."[8]

> Over the past five years, there has been a 35 percent increase in user-generated online content. Today more than 80 percent of online content is user generated.[e]

Customization

As a professor in a graduate program, I get to see a lot of engagement rings. Today, many are custom creations, something I rarely saw ten years ago. My students, full of excitement and pride, eagerly share the details of their designs. Clearly part of the thrill of their ring is in its uniqueness and the pleasure of having created it themselves.

Many consumers, particularly young adults, enjoy being part of the process of creating the products they'll own, from bicycles to running shoes. They like having something that's unique to their needs—and their tastes. As you know from earlier chapters, communicating who you are through what you own is a shorthand way to connect with others.

Consumers who are invited to play and create on websites and apps develop a deeper relationship with the brands that have facilitated the experience. They're investing time and imagination, which facilitates an emotional connection to the brand. What might start as configuring a dream car, couch, or earrings for fun can easily develop into a goal. In other words, the creative play of trying out different frames on photos, fabric combinations on furniture, or fake eyelashes on your virtual photo can easily turn into a purchase.

Glasses.com is an online-only retailer with a virtual reality app that allows users to upload a video of their face at different angles and then "try on" glasses using their 3-D image. You can even slide the glasses down your virtual nose—which is how many of us end up wearing them anyway. Glasses.com hardly needs to advertise: users can send photos of themselves to friends, who can then vote—and are likely to become engaged themselves. As Richard Mullins, author of a *Tampa Tribune* article on Glasses.com, points out, "I wasn't even looking for new glasses, but the app sure has me thinking now."[9]

Crowdsourcing

Lay's "Do Us a Flavor" campaign generated 3.8 million submissions. There's no focus group facilitator on earth who could generate that many new ideas. Of course many of the submissions, like "possum hash," probably wouldn't have made it to the testing phase. But Lay's didn't limit online input to suggesting flavors. Through a variety of social media venues such as Twitter hashtag entries and an "I'd Eat That" button on Lay's Facebook app, consumers could weigh in on which flavors they liked. Cheesy Garlic Bread beat out cofinalists Sriracha and Chicken & Waffles to earn its creator a $1 million prize. In other countries, Sunday Roast and Pickled Cucumber were the winning new flavors. So engaged were consumers that leftover bags of the runner-up flavors were going for $14 apiece on Amazon.

Part crowdsourcing, part contest, Lay's campaign captured the interest, imagination, and attention of many consumers around the world. Young adults in particular were eager to participate, keeping a mature brand like Lay's fresh in the eyes of young consumers. Beyond all the attention and publicity, Lay's campaign generated involvement—which is an investment of emotional energy that connects brands with consumers.

Our ability to harvest the opinions of our consumers in order to extend, develop, and refine brand offerings is an unmistakable opportunity. Caterpillar, maker of equipment like backhoe loaders and hydraulic excavators, actually crowdsourced a truck. Through their online customer research panel, Caterpillar incorporated the input of vocational truck users throughout the development stage of a new multipurpose truck. And Samuel Adams Brewery created a new beer, right down to the color, yeast, malt, and hops, through crowdsourcing.

One of the original crowdsourcing companies is the online clothing retailer Threadless. What started in 2000 as a simple T-shirt design contest turned into what *Inc.* magazine called "the most innovative small company in America." The 2.5 million members of the Threadless community create and submit designs, vote on designs, buy designs, and, more recently, play around on their website and attend online and in-person events. In addition to T-shirts, Threadless manufactures winning designs on products like phone cases and wall art.

The inspiration and engagement of crowdsourcing makes consumers into co-owners of the brand, rendering old-school persuasion tactics irrelevant. Harley-Davidson sums it up in their ad for their 2014 crowdsourced motorcycle: "Built by all of us. For all of us. The next Harley-Davidson."[10]

Contests

It's human to want to play games—to engage, compete, and be challenged. Although winning is wonderful, the process of playing is also satisfying because it fuels our imaginations and connects us with others. Even though other players might be "the enemy," we still have a sense of common purpose and belonging.

When it comes to brand-sponsored contests, the prospect of winning a prize is usually the impetus to play. But not so for Monopoly, the 110-year-old board game. More than ten million people voted in a Facebook contest to determine which Monopoly board piece would be retired and what new piece would be added. (The iron was fired, and a cat was added to the lineup.)

What made this contest especially effective was the participation of other brands. For example, Zappos campaigned to keep the boot, and 9Lives encouraged votes to add the new cat board piece. Their participation and highly engaging Facebook posts created an imaginary community of humanized brands. Hasbro said the contest was "tremendously successful" and that it contributed to a boost in sales.

The fame game mentioned in Chapter Two is a perfect match for contests. American Eagle Outfitters tapped into the aspirations of nearly eighty thousand people hoping to see themselves on the big screen—literally. Finalists had their photos displayed on the giant twenty-five-story LED screen outside the American Eagle flagship store in Times Square. Seven winners received $3,000 each, and two hundred finalists received a $100 American Eagle gift card. With paltry prize money like that on the table, obviously the real prize was fame. The contest generated interest and enthusiasm well beyond the eighty thousand hopefuls. More than half a million people viewed photos of contestants. Online view time collectively topped forty years over the four-week voting period. [11]

•••

When brands and retailers involve their customers with their products through their use of the four C's, they showcase their authority and demonstrate a passion for what they're selling. They're florists who love flowers a bit more, they're dance stores that care more about dance, and they're manufacturers with a little more knowledge about engineering. These brands and retailers are therefore more credible and trustworthy because they're not just about the sale—they've proven their devotion to a higher purpose. It's about the products—not the selling. So when Deb's Dance Boutique asks Facebook fans to vote on which costume a local favorite should wear, or posts videos on their website of customers competing, they communicate involvement and dedication that translates into more involved and devoted customers.

7

Intensity

The new consumer brain, discussed in Chapter One, gets bored and distracted easily. Ambiguity and complexity require focus—and that's at a premium today. Brands and retailers have to ramp up the amount of stimulus they put out around their products in order to get their share of attention. They not only have to know more quickly and completely what consumers need and want but also have to find faster, more exciting, more efficient, and more satisfying ways to provide the fulfillment of those needs and wants. You might say it takes a lot of bang to get a buck today.

Take a classic giveaway promotion: the first one hundred customers will get a free T-shirt! Pretty limp, right? Though "free" is still the four-letter word that always gets a rise out of consumers, a T-shirt is unlikely to motivate a 'round-the-block lineup. Desigual has managed to get hundreds of shoppers in locations around the globe to line up overnight—sometimes even in the rain—for their freebie. How? They've ramped it up. The Desigual promotion requires shoppers to arrive in their underwear. The first one hundred get a free top and bottom of their choice. So why would hundreds more stand in line? Because it's a party. It's exciting and a little daring. It's a natural for Instagram and Twitter. It's about social satisfaction even more than it's about scoring swag.

Simply put, it takes more to break through to busy brains. Not only are we *not* bothered by interruptions, but our brains have come to look forward to distractions. We crave stimulation in real life that replicates the constant and intense stimulation of online content and the buzzes and bings of our smartphones.

So, what's a retailer or brand to do? Let me share with you some tactics that have worked for retailers and brands or have won over some of the consumers I've interviewed.

BREAKTHROUGH MESSAGING

Communication with a kick, the kind that engages the recipient as much as the sender, has emotional intensity and personal relevance.

Talk Like Me

Research shows that when people view Web pages, they don't really read. They scan in quick cursory patterns, digesting bits and pieces of information as they go. Much of the information and the perceptions they acquire are their fast take on the images and symbolism on the page. In other words, words are blah blah blah.

Consumers, especially younger ones who have grown up with the Internet, read instruction manuals, package copy, and advertising the same way. Blocks of copy can still be meaningful, but not for what's contained within the words. Instead, people pick up on the symbolism, what a block of copy might mean—that something is complicated or detailed or researched. If that's not the message you hope to communicate, it's time to rethink messaging. In addition, and often instead of the words that are chosen, it's the gestalt of the page or website that matters. The whole is greater than the sum of the parts. I recently received a promotional mailer with a big block of words describing the creativity and excitement of an upcoming event the sender hoped I would attend. More effective would have been a genuinely creative layout, and photos of all the excitement I missed at last year's event. Showing—not telling—is increasingly how people communicate. So "talking like me" means attending to the total visual image of communication, not just what the words say.

Make It About Me

Radical individualism, of the kind we discussed at length in Chapter Two, demands relevance. When I asked Ruby to tell me about a positive retail experience, she thought for a minute and said, "I got an email from Nordstrom that really caught my eye. It said, 'Your items will arrive soon, Ruby.' I don't know why that sort of made me smile."

I think I might. It's because normally online retailers say, "We've shipped your items." It's a subtle difference that represents a big shift from "what *we're* doing" to "what *you're* getting." It made Ruby smile, and it stood out to her. Most people won't consciously register the new, more consumer-centric wording. But they will register it emotionally and then transfer that emotion to the retailer.

Consumers are relying on brands and retailers to translate product characteristics into emotional benefits. The more extraordinary those emotional benefits, the better. When anxiety, radical individualism, and limited attention come together, what's emotionally extraordinary is escape, power, control, simplicity, and centrality.

To be suspended in time in a more interesting place, to feel allowed to break the rules or be self-indulgent, or to be transformed into someone with perfect power and control—these are some of the fantasies that excite overloaded, individualistic minds. Fantasies are a peephole into consumer cravings. It's easy to see the appeal of what's popular now: vampire and serial-killer dramas that are a momentary escape into a world of rule bending and power; period dramas with their anxiety-reducing etiquette and social rules; and reality programming, which is relaxing because by comparison we're reassured that we're doing OK. The common thread among each of these is the awe that comes from seeing people connect against all odds—because as we know, connection is the most potent of all human needs.

Retailers and brands that reinterpret these fantasies or themes into benefits and emotional moments for consumers give them a bit of what they're craving most. Jessica described a recent retail experience: "I love the overall aesthetic of the All Saints store in Soho. It's industrial and rugged and beautiful—dark wood and vintage sewing machines lining the wall—and then the softest sweater in the world on the rack right in front of it. It's a place I like to just walk around and be in. Every detail in that store contributes. It's another world. It's cool."

Kiehl's has turned skin-care shopping into an adventure. Some locations feature curiosities such as old-fashioned dispensing machines; others have soda fountains and photo booths. The employees in their white lab coats give customers the sense that they've been transported to an old-fashioned chemistry lab rather than a store. "Perhaps it's the white lab coat, but they're always showing off new products and mixing up samples to send home with you," explained Abby. "They're so low key, no pressure. It's like asking the chemist for advice, not being sold." It's a triple whammy: an *attention*-worthy journey to a more *trustworthy* time, with a *science* theme.

Häagen-Dazs ice cream has always had just five ingredients. But their Five Simple Ingredients packaging and campaign boosted the popularity of the brand. The same goes for Lay's Potato Chips, which touts "three simple ingredients." Purity and simplicity are highly resonant virtues that, ironically for ice cream and potato chips, translate emotionally into a sense of control, which makes indulgence and rule breaking emotionally more acceptable.

Surprise Me

What do Costco, flash sales, pop-up stores, and slot machines have in common? That's right! Intermittent reinforcement schedules— the most intoxicating and addictive kind of "win" the human brain can process. If you got a reward every time you did something, it would be called a paycheck. And you would pretty quickly stop thinking of it as a reward and come to expect it. Can you imagine anyone playing a slot machine if he knew that every fifth spin of the wheel would be a "win" that would return 90 percent of what he gambled? That's about how slot machines actually work—with one big exception. The 90 percent repayment is awarded in varying sums and on an unpredictable schedule—otherwise known as an intermittent reinforcement schedule.

The exciting flutter of emotion that shoppers feel when they stumble across an unexpected treasure at Costco or their favorite brand in a flash sale is entirely related to the fact that they *don't* find a special treasure every single time they go to Costco or shop that flash sale.

I'm not suggesting that retailers should hold back on offering great products. Rather, I'm suggesting that retailers build in unexpected rewards to ramp up the impact of shopping. Jay was thrilled when he received his Zappos purchase. "They included a little note saying they'd upgraded my shipping to overnight!" The surprise could be a little gift, a limited cache of special products, or a mini pop-up venue related to a cultural trend, band, or seasonal color. The food truck concept has moved beyond food: things like fashion boutiques, cigar lounges, shoe repair stores, and karaoke bars are heading to the streets, where they're noticed. They're convenient *and* engaging—a surprising and captivating eruption of retail spaces into public places.

Big, immobile stores can surprise and delight consumers, too, usually by rotating inventory out quickly or offering special products at particular times. "I love shopping at Costco the most during the holidays because they have these special extra things," says Angelica. "I got my husband a snakeskin belt last year. I'm still hoping someday they might bring back these tulips that you can watch grow in a glass jar. It's always an adventure there. Plus I get my regular groceries too." Chantell recalls, "On my way to Trader Joe's, I passed by Ross and saw a cute dress in the window. I like Macy's, so I had never been in before. I ended up actually buying the dress and also some sunglasses and a bath rug. They were all things I'd needed, and they were like 80 percent off. Then the next day I went back to see if I missed anything. And then the next week I was back again. I think I'm addicted to hunting for deals there."

There's another reason why surprises are important: habituation. We don't focus as intently on things that are expected and familiar. Once our brain becomes accustomed to seeing something, we don't really see it anymore. Surprise breaks through, and as an added benefit, we're more likely to remember surprising experiences.

Jayne O'Donnell, the consumer and retail reporter for *USA Today*, notes another reason for the allure of novelty and surprise, which is that "short attention spans crave new things." O'Donnell says that stores which constantly update, rotate, and refresh their merchandise satisfy our younger generations of shoppers in particular. "They want the newest and the latest. They fly from one style to the next."[1] That's one of the reasons why "fast fashion," with its constantly rejuvenated selection, has been so successful.

Shock Me

One more tactic to break through and get attention is to shock, amuse, and otherwise engage the brain. Mildly shocking or transgressive messaging transforms the boring or mundane into a titillating experience that both captures attention and generates the "rub-off" effect mentioned in Chapter Six, whereby your brand or message gets a boost from the feelings your delivery generates.

A notable (or notorious) recent entry in the "shock me" category is Kmart's "Ship My Pants," which garnered twenty million YouTube views within four months of posting. It's an expertly performed scatological giggle that also manages to make the point that Kmart offers free shipping for items not available in the stores. The ad starts with a customer replying to a Kmart salesperson's news of free shipping with, "I just might ship my pants!" (Say it quickly if you haven't gotten the joke yet.) It follows with other shoppers saying they plan to ship their drawers, nightgowns, and beds, and an older shopper who says, "I just shipped my pants, and it's very convenient." The video got attention and humanized Kmart. It was a daring play for Kmart, but YouTube thumbs-up votes outnumbered thumbs-down votes by a ratio of 25 to 1.

These days, we're a jalapeño martini society that craves an extra boost of stimulation. It simply takes more to break through in order to capture and hold consumers' attention: more personal attention, more world building and magic making, more layers of reward, more wit, and more excitement.

EASY DOES IT

Although it's true that more really is more for today's shopper, the reverse is also true in a sense. It can seem that shoppers are of two minds: they want to stumble across treasures, to be surprised by unexpected treats, and to sample exciting new flavors. But they also want fast, trustworthy, well-organized products and retail experiences that are intensely satisfying in their simplicity and purity. In other words, they want the intensity of a jalapeño martini in a single-serving, ready-to-pour bottle.

> In the past decade, the ten fastest-growing food categories are all rip-open-and-eat types of things, like nuts and chips. Food manufacturers are creating products like pre-syruped waffle bars that you can eat with your hands and yogurt you can eat on the run by squeezing it out of a tube.[a]

Help Me Multitask

CNBC consumer reporter Kelli Grant tweeted, "There is a Black-Friday-esque line outside of Petco which opens at 10 on Sunday."

The reason? A pet clinic. Multitasking retail outlets have gone way beyond shoeshines in men's departments—and consumers love the convenience. Whether they're picking up dry cleaning at train stations or getting flu shots at Walgreens, consumers are truly appreciative of combined services.

More restaurants are featuring gift shops, and not just for take-home desserts. Aside from the convenience, unexpected products get more than their fair share of attention. The Bachelor Farmer restaurant in Minneapolis has an adjoining retail shop that sells everything from menswear to toys.[2] Mindy told me about a baking dish she was inspired to purchase at Crate & Barrel after enjoying a meal at an upscale restaurant. When I asked her if she would have bought it at the restaurant, she said, "Absolutely. I would have paid more, too, because I would have been sure it was the right kind." Her husband, Chester, who was listening in, added, "You know what I'd really love to see is a car mechanic at the airport parking garage."

Multitasking products also make sense to multitasking consumers. After all, if smartphones can do it all, why not a blanket that's also a sweatshirt? It goes by the name of Snuggie. Or a solar-powered bikini that can charge your cellphone? Workout wear is an especially ambitious category that includes clothing that is odor reducing or sweat reducing (or amplifying, depending on your needs), that has UV protection built in, or that generates heat or attacks cellulite while you work out. Although these products are more complicated with all those added extras, to the consumer they're time savers, life *simplifiers*, and just plain more interesting.

Help Me Keep It Simple

Our brains don't like complexity—and that's never been more true than today. We naturally gravitate toward simple answers, mental shortcuts, and fast solutions. Today those human instincts are ramped up by mental overload.

Simple, intuitively understood products, processes, and transactions calm anxiety, reduce boredom, and make shoppers feel central and important. Consumers also want products and retail experiences that have been stripped free of time-consuming, irritating, or cumbersome barriers: parking problems, complicated store or website navigation, lengthy instruction manuals, slow checkout procedures, and the like.

> Nearly 10 percent of Starbucks store transactions are made through their fast, easy mobile payment app.[b]

Take Silvercar as an example. Silvercar is a service that's recently entered a few markets, including Dallas and San Francisco. You get one car to choose from, a silver Audi A4. Because there's only one car, there's only one price. There are no options; it automatically comes with satellite radio and Wi-Fi. It's refilled when you return it at the local going rate for gas plus $5.00. Tolls are tracked automatically and added to your bill. Reservations and billing are completed through the Silvercar app that you download to your smartphone. Once you've completed a profile and provided credit information, you pick up your car by taking a picture of a QR code on the windshield of the car, and off you go. The big differences are less waiting upon check-in or return, a technology-loaded car, and no choices to make. For some, it's impersonal and bereft of options—for others, it's the simplicity they crave.

We love it when retailers anticipate the default options that match our needs and automatically select what we're most likely to want rather than forcing us to use precious brain energy choosing every feature. Of course we also like control, so the ability to reselect later is also appreciated. Silvercar is the ultimate in preselected default options for car rental.

• • •

Our use of technology has dramatically changed how we process information. Therefore, marketers hoping to be heard will have to communicate differently. For one thing, it simply takes more oomph to break through and get attention. Consumers won't wade through irrelevant information, lengthy explanations, or anything that doesn't seem immediately important or interesting. They require emotional relevance, intensity, and anxiety-reducing simplicity.

Conclusion

My earliest interest as a research psychologist was to understand how top marketers went about solving business problems. In my research, I found that the process followed a typical path. It started with an intense period of immersion into the facts and objectives of the project. Next, the marketers trusted their unconscious minds to harvest solutions and ideas. I'm not saying there wasn't a bit of angst accompanying that trust, but most seemed to understand that logic and thinking alone weren't going to produce results. The answers had to come from parts of their mind that they could feed with ideas but couldn't necessarily control.

An interesting tidbit surfaced in my research that opened my eyes to the importance of consumer psychology. Nearly all of the top performers I studied had gone through an experience as a child that caused them to want to understand people. For example, they had moved more than once, had a sibling who was ill, or had witnessed a disturbing event. As a result of their experience, they became a little more vigilant in studying how humans worked. The intense interest they had in understanding people contributed to what appeared to be magical solutions to business problems.

It's long been clear that the more marketers know about people, the better they'll be at their jobs. That knowledge has typically been limited to what consumers say or how they behave. I wanted to use my training in clinical psychology to take you further—to give you more useful insights—because the secret to decoding the consumer mind is in understanding that the most important calculations of every purchase decision and brand relationship occur in the deep, unconscious recesses of the mind.

Consumers are radically different than they were just a few short years ago, not just in how they behave, but in how they think, feel, and relate. Purchases and brand relationships are determined by a complex web of psychological factors. There is no single influence, no one answer. The solution for marketers is to deeply understand the new motivating factors and psychology of consumers as fuel for new ideas. And that's what I hope I've given you here. The tactics and strategies in this book are for inspiration; they're not the one answer. The answer is percolating in your unconscious mind right this minute.

Notes

Introduction

1. Meg James, "Omnicom, Publicis Merging to Create Global Advertising Behemoth," *Los Angeles Times*, July 28, 2013, http://articles.latimes .com/2013/jul/28/entertainment/la-et-ct-advertising-behemoth-created -by-omnicom-publicis-merger-20130728.

2. Melissa Lavigne-Delville, "Five Unexpected Ways Brands Can Benefit from Today's Auction Economy," *Forbes*, March 1, 2012, http://www .forbes.com/sites/forbeswomanfiles/2012/03/01/five-unexpected-ways -brands-can-benefit-from-todays-online-auction-economy/.

3. *The Harris Poll RQ Summary Report*, Harris Interactive, February 2013, http://www.harrisinteractive.com/vault/2013%20RQ%20Summary%20 Report%20FINAL.pdf.

Chapter 1

1. "2012 State of the Industry: Energy Drinks," *Beverage Industry*, July 18, 2012, http://www.bevindustry.com/articles/85663-2012-state-of-the -industry-report?v=preview.

2. Maureen Mackey, "Sleepless in America: A $32.4 Billion Business," *Fiscal Times*, July 23, 2012, http://www.thefiscaltimes.com/Articles/2012/07/23 /Sleepless-in-America-A-32-4-Billion-Business.

3. Wendy Liebmann, CEO, WSL Strategic, personal interview with Kit Yarrow, June 19, 2013.

4. Kelly Mooney (CEO, Resource), opening remarks, Resource Open Brand Summit, Columbus, Ohio, May 9, 2013.

5. Steve McClellan, "Kids to Marketers: We Want Tech Gadgets, Not Toys." *MediaDailyNews*, March 13, 2013, http://www.mediapost.com /publications/article/195747/.

6. Judith Newman, "Appily Ever After: A Smartphone Shrink," *New York Times*, April 5, 2013, http://forum.psychlinks.ca/computers-technology -and-the-internet/31424-appily-ever-after-a-smartphone-shrink.html.

7. "BrandZ Top 100 Global Brands: Take Aways," Millward Brown (May 2012), http://www.millwardbrown.com/BrandZ/Top_100_Global_Brands /Take_Aways.aspx.

8. Clayton Christensen, *The Innovator's Dilemma: The Revolutionary New Book That Will Change the Way You Do Business* (New York: HarperBusiness, 2011).

9. John Digles, executive VP and general manager, MWW, personal interview with Kit Yarrow, May 13, 2013.

10. Courtney Reagan, "Coming to a Store Near You: Cutting-Edge Technology," CNBC (August 20, 2013), http://www.cnbc.com /id/100975288.

11. "Edelman Trust Barometer: 2012 Annual Global Study," Edelman (2012), http://trust.edelman.com.

12. Keller Fay Group, "Nearly a Trillion Conversations!" www.kellerfay.com.

13. "Nielsen: Global Consumers' Trust in 'Earned' Advertising Grows in Importance," Nielsen (April 10, 2012), http://www.nielsen.com/us/en /press-room/2012/nielsen-global-consumers-trust-in-earned-advertising -grows.html.

14. Wildfire by Google, "Engaging Consumers Where It Matters Most," Wildfire Interactive (2013), http://go.wf-social.com/rs/wildfire/images /wp_customer%20lifecycle_f.pdf.

15. Lev Muchnik, Sinan Aral, and Sean J. Taylor, "Social Influence Bias: A Randomized Experiment," *Science* 341, no. 6146 (August 9, 2013): 647–651.

16. Alyson Shontell, "Angry Customer Buys Promoted Tweets to Bash British Airways for Losing His Luggage," *Business Insider*, September 3, 2013, http://www.businessinsider.com/customer-buys-promoted-tweets-to-bash -british-airways-2013-9.

17. Steph Lippitt, "Eight Secrets to a Successful Kickstarter Campaign," FindSpark (April 25, 2012), http://www.findspark.com/2012/04/25 /eight-secrets-to-a-successful-kickstarter-campaign/.

18. Sarah Oliver, owner, Sarah Oliver Handbags, personal interview with Kit Yarrow, August 31, 2013.

19. Gary Small, *iBrain: Surviving the Technological Alteration of the Modern Mind* (New York: William Morrow, 2008).

20. "Email's Dark Side: 10 Psychology Studies," PsyBlog (September 1, 2010), http://www.spring.org.uk/2010/09/emails-dark-side-10-psychology-studies .php.

21. Sarah Nassauer, "The Art of Almost Homemade," *Wall Street Journal*, June 18, 2013, http://online.wsj.com/news/articles/SB1000142412788732 4021104578553570654727736.

22. "Even Brief Interruptions Spawn Errors," *ScienceDaily*, January 7, 2013, http://www.sciencedaily.com/releases/2013/01/130107100059.htm.

23. Bianca Bosker, "Clifford Nass on 'Seductive' Tech and Why You Treat Your Phone Like a Friend," *Huffington Post*, March 6, 2013, http://www .huffingtonpost.com/2013/03/03/clifford-nass_n_2792780.html.

24. "What Was I Doing? Interruptions Can Change Purchase Decisions," *ScienceDaily*, September 18, 2008, http://www.sciencedaily.com /releases/2008/09/080915170747.htm.

25. Thomas T. Hills, Takao Noguchi, and Michael Gibbert, "Information Overload or Search-Amplified Risk? Set Size and Order Effects on Decisions from Experience," *Psychonomic Bulletin & Review* 20, no. 5 (October 2013):1023–1031, doi: 10.3758/s13423-013-0422-3.

26. "Consumers Crave Simplicity Not Engagement," Corporate Executive Board (May 2012), http://news.executiveboard.com/index .php?s=23330&item=128138.

27. E. J. Schults, "Pop Psychology: Ready-Made Popcorn Gains on Microwave Brands," *Advertising Age*, May 29, 2013, http://adage.com/article/news /ready-made-popcorn-gains-microwave-brands/241686/.

28. Kelly Mooney, Resource Open Brand Summit.

29. "Just One Second Delay in Page-Load Can Cause 7% Loss in Customer Conversions," TagMan (blog), March 14, 2012, http://www.tagman.com /mdp-blog/2012/03/just-one-second-delay-in-page-load-can-cause-7-loss -in-customer-conversions/.

30. Sam McNerney, "To Benefit from Technology, We Need to Understand Psychology," Moments of Genius (Big Think blog), July 25, 2013, http://bigthink.com/insights-of-genius/to-benefit-from-technology-we -need-to-understand-psychology.

31. Sandy Smith, "Moving Fast," NRF *Stores* (May 2013), http://www.stores .org/STORES%20Magazine%20May%202013/moving-fast.

32. Kyle Stock, "Why Patagonia Wants to Sell You Ratty Old Swim Trunks," *BloombergBusinessweek*, September 25, 2013,

http://www.businessweek.com/articles/2013-09-25/why-patagonia
-wants-to-sell-you-ratty-old-swim-trunks.

33.   Paula Haerr, interim executive director, Connect2One, personal interview with Kit Yarrow, June 15, 2013.

34.   Rebecca Grant, "Wanelo 3.0 Makes E-Commerce Less 'Primitive' by Organizing Products Around People," VentureBeat (May 7, 2013), http://venturebeat.com/2013/05/07/wanelo-3-0-makes-e-commerce-less -primitive-by-organizing-products-around-people/.

35.   Lauren I. Labrecque and George R. Milne, "Exciting Red and Competent Blue: The Importance of Color in Marketing," *Journal of the Academy of Marketing Science* 40, no. 5 (September 2012): 711–726.

36.   Betina Piqueras-Fiszman and Charles Spence, "The Influence of the Color of the Cup on Consumers' Perception of a Hot Beverage," *Journal of Sensory Studies* 27, no. 5 (2012): 324, doi: 10.1111/j.1745-459X.2012.00397.x.

37.   Rajesh Bagchi and Amar Cheema, "The Effect of Red Background Color on Willingness-to-Pay: The Moderating Role of Selling Mechanism," *Journal of Consumer Research* 39, no. 5 (February 2013), doi:10.1086/666466.

38.   Nicolas Guéguen and Céline Jacob, "Clothing Color and Tipping: Gentlemen Patrons Give More Tips to Waitresses with Red Clothes," *Journal of Hospitality & Tourism Research*, April 18, 2012, http://jht .sagepub.com/content/early/2012/04/16/1096348012442546.

39.   Joshua Porter, "The Button Color A/B Test: Red Beats Green," HubSpot blog, August 2, 2011, http://blog.hubspot.com/blog/tabid/6307/bid/20566 /The-Button-Color-A-B-Test-Red-Beats-Green.aspx.

40.   Brad Tuttle, "Wine Drinkers Will Pay More for Bottles with Hard-to-Pronounce Names," *TIME*, June 27, 2012, http://business.time .com/2012/06/27/wine-drinkers-pay-more-for-bottles-with-hard-to -pronounce-names/.

41.   Keith S. Coulter, "Comma N' Cents in Pricing: The Effects of Auditory Representation Encoding on Price Magnitude Perceptions," *Journal of Consumer Psychology* 22, no. 3 (July 1, 2012): 395–407.

42.   Wan-chen Lee, Jenny Mitsuru Shimizu, Kevin M. Kniffin, and Brian Wansink, "You Taste What You See: Do Organic Labels Bias Taste Perceptions?" *Food Quality and Preference* 29, no. 1 (2013): 33–39, doi: 10.1016/j.foodqual.2013.01.010.

43.   John A. Bargh, Mark Chen, and Lara Burrows, "Automaticity of Social Behavior: Direct Effects of Trait Construct and Stereotype-Activation on

Action," *Journal of Personality and Social Psychology* 71 (1996): 230–244, doi:10.1037//0022-3514.71.2.230.

44. A. Selin Atalay, H. Onur Bodur, and Dina Rasolofoarison, "Shining in the Center: Central Gaze Cascade Effect on Product Choice," *Journal of Consumer Research* 39, no. 4 (December 2012): 848–866.

45. Bruce D. Sanders, Ph.D., author, *Retailer's Edge*, personal interview with Kit Yarrow, May 20, 2013.

46. Richard E. Nisbett and Timothy Decamp Wilson, "Telling More Than We Can Know: Verbal Reports on Mental Processes," *Psychological Review* 84, no. 3 (1977): 231–259.

47. Boyoun Chae, Xiuping Li, and Rui Zhu, "Judging Product Effectiveness from Perceived Spatial Proximity," *Journal of Consumer Research* 40, no. 2 (August 2013): 317–335.

48. Rob Holland, Merel Hendriks, and Henk Aarts, "Smells Like Clean Spirit: Nonconscious Effects of Scent on Cognition and Behavior," *Psychological Science* 16, no. 9 (2006): 689–693.

49. Ibid.

50. Nicolas Gueguen and Christine Petr, "Odors and Consumer Behavior in a Restaurant," *International Journal of Hospitality Management* 25 (2006): 335–339.

51. Kristin McCombs, Bryan Raudenbush, Andrea Bova, and Mark Sappington, "Effects of Peppermint Scent Administration on Cognitive Video Game Performance," *North American Journal of Psychology* 13, no. 3 (2011): 383.

52. Harris Interactive, "Americans Can't Put Down Their Smartphones, Even During Sex," Jumio (July 11, 2013), http://www.jumio.com/2013/07/americans-cant-put-down-their-smartphones-even-during-sex/.

53. World Internet Project, *World Internet Project International Report: Third Edition 2012*, Center for the Digital Future (December 2012), http://www.digitalcenter.org/wp-content/uploads/2012/12/2012wip_report3rd_ed.pdf.

54. Sam Laird, "Social Networks: Are They Eroding Our Social Lives?" Mashable (April 25, 2012), http://mashable.com/2012/04/25/social-networks-study/.

55. Kevin Fitchard, "2013: The Year Mobile Data Revenue Will Eclipse Voice in US," GIGAOM (March 13, 2013), http://gigaom.com/2013/03/13/2013-the-year-mobile-data-revenue-will-eclipse-voice-in-the-us/.

56. "The 2013 Digital Marketer Report," Experian Marketing Services. Available at http://www.experian.com/marketing-services/2013-digital-marketer-report.html.

57.   David Carr, "Keep Your Thumbs Still When I'm Talking to You," *New York Times*, April 15, 2011, http://www.nytimes.com/2011/04/17 /fashion/17TEXT.html?pagewanted=all&_r=0.

Chapter 1 Feature Box Source Notes

a.   Steven J. Vaughan-Nichols, "Half-a-Billion Internet-Connected Devices and Counting," *ZDNet*, March 21, 2013, http://www.zdnet.com /half-a-billion-internet-connected-devices-and-counting-7000012958/.

b.   Gartner Webinars, "By 2017 the CMO Will Spend More on IT Than the CIO" (January 3, 2012), http://my.gartner.com/portal/server.pt?open=512 &objID=202&mode=2&PageID=5553&resId=1871515.

c.   John Cacioppo, Stephanie Cacioppo, Gian C. Gonzaga, Elizabeth L. Ogburn, and Tyler J. VanderWeele, "Marital Satisfaction and Break-Ups Differ Across On-Line and Off-Line Meeting Venues," *Proceedings of the National Academy of Sciences of the United States of America* (May 31, 2013), http://www.pnas.org/content/early/2013/05/31/1222447110.full .pdf.

d.   "Statistics," YouTube, http://www.youtube.com/yt/press/statistics.html.

e.   Mark Walsh, "Microsoft Highlights Usage Across Device 'Pathways,'" *OnlineMediaDaily*, March 15, 2013, http://www.mediapost.com/ publications/article/195786/#axzz2afQZKFPQ.

f.   "Tablets: Retail 2013," L2 (April 2, 2013), http://www.l2thinktank.com /research/tablets-retail-2013.

g.   Kelly Mooney, Resource Open Brand Summit.

h.   Rebecca Corless, "Photos on Facebook Generate 53% More Likes Than the Average Post," *HubSpot* (blog), November 15, 2012, http://blog .hubspot.com/blog/tabid/6307/bid/33800/Photos-on-Facebook-Generate -53-More-Likes-Than-the-Average-Post-NEW-DATA.aspx.

i.   Olga Kharif, "Shoppers' 'Mobile Blinders' Force Checkout-Aisle Changes," Bloomberg (March 21, 2013), http://www.bloomberg.com /news/2013-03-21/shoppers-mobile-blinders-force-checkout-aisle -changes.html.

Chapter 2

1.   Kelly Mooney (CEO, Resource), opening remarks, Resource Open Brand Summit, Columbus, Ohio, May 9, 2013.

2.   Donghee Yvette Wohn, Nicole B. Ellison, M. Laeeq Khan, Ryan Fewins-Bliss, and Rebecca Gray, "The Role of Social Media in Shaping First-Generation High School Students' College Aspirations: A Social

Capital Lens," *Computers & Education* 63 (April 2013): 424–436, doi:10.1016/j.compedu.2013.01.004.

3. John Helliwell and Haifang Huang, "Comparing the Happiness Effects of Real and On-line Friends," NBER Working Paper No. 18690, National Bureau of Economic Research (January 2013), http://www.nber.org/papers/w18690.

4. Carl G. Jung, *Two Essays on Analytical Psychology* (London: Rutledge & Kegan Paul, 1953), 190.

5. Sherry Turkle, "The Flight from Conversation," *New York Times*, April 21, 2012, http://www.nytimes.com/2012/04/22/opinion/sunday/the-flight-from-conversation.html?_r=0.

6. Nick Summers, "Dating App Tinder Catches Fire," *BloombergBusinessweek*, September 5, 2013, http://www.businessweek.com/articles/2013-09-05/dating-app-tinder-catches-fire.

7. Brené Brown, *Daring Greatly: How the Courage to Be Vulnerable Transforms the Way We Live, Love, Parent, and Lead* (New York: Gotham, 2012).

8. SunWolf, Ph.D., professor of communication, Santa Clara University, personal interview with Kit Yarrow, May 20, 2013.

9. Jason Dubroy, VP managing director, shopper marketing, DDB Canada, personal interview with Kit Yarrow, May 13, 2013.

10. Jake Halpern, *Fame Junkies* (Boston: Houghton Mifflin, 2007).

11. Yalda T. Uhls and Patricia M. Greenfield, "The Value of Fame: Preadolescent Perceptions of Popular Media and Their Relationship to Future Aspirations," *Developmental Psychology* 48, no. 2 (March 2012): 315–326, doi: 10.1037/a0026369.

12. Yalda T. Uhls and Patricia M. Greenfield, "The Rise of Fame: An Historical Content Analysis," *Cyberpsychology: Journal of Psychosocial Research on Cyberspace* 5, no. 1, article 1 (2011), http://www.cyberpsychology.eu/view.php?cisloclanku=2011061601.

13. "Millennials: A Portrait of "Generation Next," Pew Research Center (2007), http://www.pewresearch.org/millennials/.

14. Yalda T. Uhls, PhD, regional director, Common Sense Media, personal interview with Kit Yarrow, June 16, 2013.

15. Greg Berardi, founder and chief marketing strategist, Blue Marlin Partners, personal interview with Kit Yarrow, May 10, 2013.

16. David Brooks, "What Our Words Tell Us," *New York Times*, May 20, 2013, http://www.nytimes.com/2013/05/21/opinion/brooks-what-our-words-tell-us.html?_r=0.

17.   Joseph Stromberg, "Eric Klinenberg on Going Solo," *Smithsonian*, February 2012, http://www.smithsonianmag.com/science-nature/Eric -Klinenberg-on-Going-Solo.html.

18.   Rocio Calvo, Yuhui Zheng, Santosh Kumar, Analia Olgiati, and Lisa Berkman, "Well-Being and Social Capital on Planet Earth: Cross-National Evidence from 142 Countries," *PLOS ONE*, August 15, 2012, http://www.plosone.org/article/info%3Adoi%2F10.1371%2Fjournal .pone.0042793; John Helliwell, Haifan Huang, and Shun Wang, "Social Capital and Well-Being in Times of Crisis," *Journal of Happiness Studies*, May 2013, http://faculty.arts.ubc.ca/jhelliwell/papers/Helliwell-Huang -Wang-JOHS2013.pdf.

19.   Jim Taylor, PhD, personal interview with Kit Yarrow, May 23, 2013.

20.   Robert Putnam, *Bowling Alone: The Collapse and Revival of American Community* (New York: Simon & Schuster, 2000).

21.   Miller McPherson, Lynn Smith-Lovin, and Matthew E. Brashears, "Social Isolation in America: Changes in Core Discussion Networks over Two Decades," *American Sociological Review* 71, no. 3 (2006): 353–375.

22.   Jeanna Bryner, "Close Friends Less Common Today, Study Finds," LiveScience (November 4, 2011), http://www.livescience.com/16879 -close-friends-decrease-today.html.

23.   Scott Wiltermuth and Chip Heath, "Synchrony and Cooperation," *Psychological Science* 20, no. 1 (January 2009): 1–5.

24.   Robert W. Smith, David Faro, and Katherine A. Burson, "More for the Many: The Influence of Entitativity on Charitable Giving," *Journal of Consumer Research* 39, no. 5 (February 2013): 961–976.

25.   "77% Think That Americans Are Getting Ruder," *Rasmussen Reports*, October 17, 2013, http://www.rasmussenreports .com/public_content/lifestyle/general_lifestyle/october _2013/77_think_americans_are_getting_ruder.

26.   Chen-Bo Zhong, Vanessa K. Bohns, and Francesca Gino, "Good Lamps Are the Best Police: Darkness Increases Dishonesty and Self-Interested Behavior," *Psychological Science* 21, no. 3 (March 2010): 311–314.

27.   Stephanie Clifford and Andrew Martin, "In Time of Scrimping, Fun Stuff Is Still Selling," *New York Times*, September 23, 2011, http://www .nytimes.com/2011/09/24/business/consumers-cut-back-on-staples-but -splurge-on-indulgences.html?_r=0.

28.   Mintel Group, *Mintel Report: American Lifestyles 2013* (July 31, 2013). Available at http://www.mintel.com/en/american-lifestyles/.

29.   John Lovett, "Life Lessons in Fighting the Culture of Bullshit," *Atlantic*, May 21, 2013, http://www.theatlantic.com/politics/archive/2013/05 /life-lessons-in-fighting-the-culture-of-bullshit/276030/.

30.   "Trust in Government," Gallup (2013), http://www.gallup.com/poll/5392 /trust-government.aspx.

31.   Frank Newport, "US Satisfaction Down to 21%," Gallup (March 19, 2013), http://www.gallup.com/poll/161426/satisfaction-down.aspx.

32.   "Confidence in Institutions," Gallup (2013), http://www.gallup.com /poll/1597/confidence-institutions.aspx.

33.   Regina A. Corso, "Oil, Pharmaceutical, Health Insurance, Tobacco, Banking and Utilities Top the List of Industries That People Would Like to See More Regulated," Harris Interactive (December 18, 2012), http://www.harrisinteractive.com/NewsRoom/HarrisPolls/tabid/447 /mid/1508/articleId/1131/ctl/ReadCustom%20Default/Default.aspx.

34.   Marcus Wohlsen, "New Bank Has No Branches, Just an App—and Thinks You'll Volunteer to Pay for It," *Wired*, January 16, 2013, http://www.wired.com/business/2013/01/go-bank-pay-what-you-want/.

35.   Paco Underhill, *Why We Buy: The Science of Shopping* (New York: Simon & Schuster, 2000).

36.   Brett A. S. Martin, "A Stranger's Touch: Effects of Accidental Interpersonal Touch on Consumer Evaluations and Shopping Time," *Journal of Consumer Research* 39, no. 1 (June 2012): 174–184.

37.   Andrea C. Morales and Gavan J. Fitzsimons, "Product Contagion: Changing Consumer Evaluations Through Physical Contact with 'Disgusting' Products," *Journal of Marketing Research* 44, no. 2 (May 2007): 272–283.

38.   Fabrizio Di Muro and Theodore J. Noseworthy, "Money Isn't Everything, but It Helps If It Doesn't Look Used: How Physical Appearance of Money Influences Spending," *Journal of Consumer Research* 39 (April 2013), http://www.jcr-admin.org/files/pressPDFs/100312163624_Noseworthy _Article.pdf, doi: 10.1086/668406.

39.   Aaron Brough and Alexander Chernev, "When Opposites Detract: Categorical Reasoning and Subtractive Valuations of Product Combinations," *Journal of Consumer Research* 39, no. 2 (August 2012): 399–414.

40.   Wendy Liebmann, CEO, WSL Strategic, personal interview with Kit Yarrow, June 19, 2013.

41.   "5 Best Practices for Increasing Earned Media," Wildfire Interactive, http://go.wf-social.com/rs/wildfire/images/Wildfire%2520Report_Maximiz e%2520Earned%2520Media%2520with%2520Social.pdf.

Chapter 2 Feature Box Source Notes

a. "Digital Dating and the Catfish Phenomenon," Ypulse (February 6, 2013), http://www.ypulse.com/post/view/digital-dating-and-the-catfish -phenomenon.

b. Regina A. Corso, "Thanks to Social Networks, Americans Feel More Connected to People," Harris Interactive (October 21, 2010), http://www .harrisinteractive.com/NewsRoom/HarrisPolls/tabid/447/mid/1508 /articleId/590/ctl/ReadCustom%20Default/Default.aspx.

c. "Cosmetic Surgery National Data Bank: Statistics 2012," American Society for Aesthetic Plastic Surgery (March 2013), http://www.surgery .org/sites/default/files/ASAPS-2012-Stats.pdf.

d. Ibid.

e. "NPD Reports Annual 2011 U.S. Prestige Beauty Posts Highest Sales Results in Fifteen Years," PRWeb (March 1, 2012), http://www.prweb .com/releases/2012/3/prweb9240231.htm.

f. Nicole Granese, "From Princess to Diva: Gen We's New Beauty Culture," MediaPost (March 22, 2013), http://www.mediapost.com/publications /article/196447/from-princess-to-diva-gen-wes-new-beauty-culture .html#axzz2b8DYjjzN.

g. "The Makeup of Millennials Beauty Routine," Lab 42 (blog), May 2013, http://blog.lab42.com/the-makeup-of-millennials-beauty-routine.

h. Steve Hasker, "Using Big Data to Engage with the New Consumer," Nielsen (June 4, 2013), http://www.nielsen.com/us/en/newswire/2013 /using-big-data-to-engage-with-the-new-consumer.html.

i. "Facebook Makes Users Feel Envious, Dissatisfied: German Study Reveals Social Network's Big Role in Users' Emotional Life," *ScienceDaily*, January 21, 2013, http://www.sciencedaily.com /releases/2013/01/130121083028.htm.

j. Ethan Kross et al., "Facebook Use Predicts Declines in Subjective Well-Being in Young Adults," *PLOS ONE*, August 14, 2013, http://www .plosone.org/article/info%3Adoi%2F10.1371%2Fjournal.pone.0069841.

k. Andrew Lepp, Jacob E. Barkley, and Aryn C. Karpinski, "The relationship between cell phone use, academic performance, anxiety and satisfaction with life in college students," *Computers in Human Behavior* 31, (2014): 343.

l. Sheila Shayon, "Super Bowl Ad, Chip Contests Show PepsiCo's Deep Belief in the Crowd," brandchannel (February 5, 2013), http://www .brandchannel.com/home/post/Pepsi-Crowd-020513.aspx.

m.   Jing Wang, Rui Zhu, and Baba Shiv, "The Lonely Consumer: Loner or Conformer?" *Journal of Consumer Research* 38, no. 6 (April 2012): 1116–1128. Available at http://www.jstor.org/discover/10.1086/66155 2?uid=3739560&uid=2129&uid=2&uid=70&uid=4&uid=3739256& sid=21102847646081.

n.   Ron Duclos, Echo Wen Wan, and Yuwei Jiang, "Show Me the Honey! Effects of Social Exclusion on Financial Risk Taking," *Journal of Consumer Research* 40, no. 1 (2013): 122–135.

o.   Susan Reda, "Driving Shoppers Crazy," NRF Stores (June 2012), http://www.stores.org/STORES%20Magazine%20June%202012 /driving-shoppers-crazy.

p.   Christine Porath and Christine Pearson, "The Price of Incivility," *Harvard Business Review*, January-February 2013, http://hbr.org/2013/01 /the-price-of-incivility/.

q.   "Antisocial Networks? Hostility on Social Media Rising for 78 Percent of Users," VitalSmarts (April 2013), http://www.vitalsmarts.com/press /2013/04/antisocial-networks-hostility-on-social-media-rising-for-78 -percent-of-users/.

r.   "Buy It, Try It, Rate It: Study of Consumer Electronics Purchase Decisions in the Engagement Era," Weber Shandwick (September 2012), http://www.webershandwick.com/uploads/news/files /ReviewsSurveyReportFINAL.pdf.

s.   Craig D. Parks, Jeff Joireman, and Paul A. M. Van Lange, "Cooperation, Trust and Antagonism: How Public Goods Are Promoted," *Psychological Science in the Public Interest* 14, no. 3 (2013): 119–165.

Chapter 3

1.   Gary W. Lewandowski Jr., "Is a Bad Mood Contagious?" *Scientific American*, July 11, 2012, http://www.scientificamerican.com/article .cfm?id=is-a-bad-mood-contagious.

2.   "Brain Sets Prices with Emotional Value," *ScienceDaily*, July 3, 2013, http://www.sciencedaily.com/releases/2013/07/130702173156 .htm.

3.   C. Nathan DeWall, Richard S. Pond Jr., W. Keith Campbell, and Jean M. Twenge, "Tuning In to Psychological Change: Linguistic Markers of Psychological Traits and Emotions over Time in Popular U.S. Song Lyrics," *Psychology of Aesthetics, Creativity, and the Arts* 5, no. 3 (2011): 200–207.

4. Joel Stein, "The Me, Me, Me Generation," *TIME*, May 20, 2013, http://content.time.com/time/magazine/article/0,9171,2143001,00.html.

5. Jean M. Twenge and W. Keith Campbell, *The Narcissism Epidemic: Living in the Age of Entitlement* (New York: Atria Books, 2010).

6. "Identifying Trends in 60 Years of Oscar Speeches," *ScienceDaily*, February 19, 2013, http://www.sciencedaily.com/releases/2013/02/130219140250.htm.

7. "Majority of US Youth Prefer to Stand Out Rather Than Blend In," Marketing Charts (August 2, 2012), http://www.marketingcharts.com/wp/topics/asia-pacific/majority-of-us-youth-prefer-to-stand-out-rather-than-blend-in-22830/.

8. Jeremy Dean, "Twitter: 10 Psychological Insights," PsyBlog (August 10, 2010), http://www.spring.org.uk/2010/08/twitter-10-psychological-insights.php.

9. Jerry M. Burger and David F. Caldwell, "When Opportunity Knocks: The Effect of a Perceived Unique Opportunity on Compliance," *Group Processes & Intergroup Relations* 14, no. 5 (September 2011): 671–680, http://gpi.sagepub.com/content/14/5/671.full.pdf+html.

10. Xavier Dreze and Joseph C. Nunes, "Feeling Superior: The Impact of Loyalty Program Structure on Consumers' Perceptions of Status," *Journal of Consumer Research* 35, no. 6 (April 2009): 890–905.

11. Seung Yun Lee and Russell Seidle, "Narcissists as Consumers: The Effects of Perceived Scarcity on Processing of Product Information," *Social Behavior and Personality* 40, no. 9 (2012): 1485–1500.

12. Wendy Liebmann, CEO, WSL Strategic, personal interview with Kit Yarrow, June 19, 2013.

13. RightNow, "RightNow Study Finds Retailers Can Win Back Unhappy Customers Through Social Media," Harris Interactive (March 1, 2011), http://www.harrisinteractive.com/vault/RightNow-Retailers-Social-Media-2011-03-02.pdf.

14. William Poundstone, *Priceless: The Myth of Fair Value (and How to Take Advantage of It)* (New York: Hill and Wang, 2011).

15. Brian Wansink, Robert J. Kent, and Stephen J. Hoch, "An Anchoring and Adjustment Model of Purchase Quantity Decisions," *Journal of Marketing Research* 35 (February 1998): 71–81.

16. Daniel Kahneman, Alan B. Krueger, David Schkade, Norbert Schwarz, and Arthur A. Stone, "A Survey Method for Characterizing Daily Life Experience: The Day Reconstruction Method," *Science* 306, no. 5702 (December 3, 2004): 1776–1780.

17. Keisha M. Cutright, "The Beauty of Boundaries: When and Why We Seek Structure in Consumption," *Journal of Consumer Research* 38, no. 5 (February 2012): 775–790.

18. Shawn Gibson, owner, Teatro Verde, personal interview with Kit Yarrow, July 11, 2013.

19. Tim Kreider, *We Learn Nothing: Essays* (New York: Simon & Schuster, 2013).

20. Anne Kadet, "'Superjobs': Why You Work More, Enjoy It Less," *Wall Street Journal Online*, May 8, 2011, http://online.wsj.com/article/SB100014 24052748703859304576309533100131932.html.

21. Yangjie Gu, Simona Botti, and David Faro, "Turning the Page: The Impact of Choice Closure on Satisfaction," *Journal of Consumer Research* 40, no. 2 (August 2013): 268–283.

22. Daniel Kahneman and Amos Tversky, "Prospect Theory: An Analysis of Decision Under Risk," *Econometrica* 47, no. 2 (1979): 263–292.

23. Maya Bar-Hillel and Efrat Neter, "Why Are People Reluctant to Exchange Lottery Tickets?" *Journal of Personality and Social Psychology* 70, no. 1 (January 1996): 17–27.

24. Vladas Griskevicius, coauthor of *The Rational Animal*, personal interview with Kit Yarrow, September 5, 2013.

25. Sheena S. Iyengar and Mark R. Lepper, "When Choice Is Demotivating: Can One Desire Too Much of a Good Thing?" *Journal of Personality and Social Psychology* 79, no. 6 (2000): 995–1006.

26. Association for Psychological Science, "Happiness Has a Dark Side," press release (May 16, 2011), http://www.psychologicalscience.org/index.php /news/releases/happiness-has-a-dark-side.html.

27. Shelly B. Flagel et al., "A Selective Role for Dopamine in Stimulus–Reward Learning," *Nature* 469, no. 7328 (January 6, 2011): 53–57, doi: 10.1038/nature09588.

28. Torsten Bornemann and Christian Homburg, "Psychological Distance and the Dual Role of Price," *Journal of Consumer Research* 38, no. 3 (October 2011): 490–504.

29. "Ebates Survey: More Than Half (51.8%) of Americans Engage in Retail Therapy—63.9% of Women and 39.8% of Men Shop to Improve Their Mood," Business Wire (April 2, 2013), http://www.businesswire.com /news/home/20130402005600/en/Ebates-Survey-51.8-Americans-Engage -Retail-Therapy%E2%80%94.

30. Selin Atalay and Margaret G. Meloy, "Retail Therapy: A Strategic Effort to Improve Mood," *Psychology & Marketing* 28, no. 6 (2011): 638–659.

31.   Hajo Adam and Adam D. Galinsky, "Enclothed Cognition," *Journal of Experimental Social Psychology* 48, no. 4 (July 2012): 918–925.

32.   Omri Gillath, Angela J. Bahns, Fiona Ge, and Christian S. Crandall, "Shoes as a Source of First of Impressions," *Journal of Research in Personality* 46, no. 4 (August 2012): 423–430.

33.   Doug Stephens, author, *The Retail Revival*, personal interview with Kit Yarrow, July 11, 2013.

Chapter 3 Feature Box Source Notes

a.   Medco Health Solutions, "America's State of Mind," WHO Essential Medicines and Health Products Information Portal (November 2012), http://apps.who.int/medicinedocs/documents /s19032en/s19032en.pdf.

b.   Humphrey Taylor, "What Are We Most Angry About? The Economy, Unemployment, the Government, Taxes and Immigration," Harris Interactive (October 21, 2010), http://www.harrisinteractive.com /NewsRoom/HarrisPolls/tabid/447/mid/1508/articleId/592/ctl /ReadCustom%20Default/Default.aspx.

c.   American Psychological Association, *Stress in America: Our Health at Risk* (January 11, 2012), http://www.apa.org/news/press/releases/stress/2011 /final-2011.pdf.

d.   Harris Interactive, "Work and Well-Being Survey," APA Center for Organizational Excellence (March 2013), http://www.apaexcellence.org /assets/general/2013-work-and-wellbeing-survey-results.pdf.

e.   Peyton Craighill, "Poll: Public Sours on What 2013 Will Bring," The Fix (*Washington Post* blog), December 24, 2012, http://www.washingtonpost .com/blogs/the-fix/wp/2012/12/24/poll-public-sours-on-what-2013 -will-bring/.

f.   Allan V. Horowitz and Jerome C. Wakefield, "Our New Era of Anxiety," *Salon*, June 2, 2012, http://www.salon.com/2012/06/02 /our_new_era_of_anxiety/.

g.   "Traditional Back to School Shopping Stresses Both Parents & Kids," *Reuters*, July 18, 2013, http://www.reuters.com/article/2013/07/18 /ca-ebates-idUSnBw185329a+100+BSW20130718.

h.   Christopher J. Carpenter, "A Meta-Analysis of the Effectiveness of the 'But You Are Free' Compliance-Gaining Technique," *Communication Studies* 64, no. 1 (2013): 6–17.

i.   Ned Smith, "Shopping Poll: 76% of Women Say They're Bargain Hunters," *BusinessNewsDaily*, April 12, 2011,

http://www.businessnewsdaily.com/861-women-shoppers-bargain
-coupons-deals.html.

Chapter 4

1. Lisa Parrish, TalentBank director, Faith Popcorn's BrainReserve, personal interview with Kit Yarrow, April 17, 2013.
2. John Digles, executive vice president and general manager, MWW, personal interview with Kit Yarrow, May 13, 2013.
3. "The CMO's Guide to Big Data," 360i (November 2012), http://www.360i.com/reports/big-data/.
4. "8 Marketers Doing Big Data Right," Mashable (May 6, 2013), http://mashable.com/2013/05/06/cmo-data/.
5. Ibid.
6. "Accenture Study Shows U.S. Consumers Want a Seamless Shopping Experience Across Store, Online and Mobile That Many Retailers Are Struggling to Deliver," Accenture (April 15, 2013), http://newsroom .accenture.com/news/accenture-study-shows-us-consumers-want-a -seamless-shopping-experience-across-store-online-and-mobile-that -many-retailers-are-struggling-to-deliver.htm.
7. Ken Nisch, chairman, JGA, personal interview with Kit Yarrow, June 17, 2013.
8. "Shopper Sentiment: How Consumers Feel About Shopping In-Store, Online, and via Mobile," Nielsen (June 6, 2012), http://www.nielsen .com/us/en/newswire/2012/shopper-sentiment-how-consumers-feel-about -shopping-in-store-online-and-via-mobile.html.
9. David Hogue, former vice president of user design, Fluid, personal interview with Kit Yarrow, July 15, 2013.
10. Jason Goldberg, VP of strategy, Razorfish, personal interview with Kit Yarrow, July 8, 2013.
11. Stephan Kanlian, chairperson, Cosmetics and Fragrance Marketing and Management Program, Fashion Institute of Technology, personal interview with Kit Yarrow, July 9, 2013.
12. Jeanine Poggi, "L'Oreal Seeks Women in Unlikely Place: On Xbox," *AdAge Digital*, October 15, 2012, http://adage.com/article /digital/l-al-seeks-women-place-xbox/237556/.

Chapter 4 Feature Box Source Notes

a. Bill Siwicki, "Shoppers Would Rather Use Smartphones Than Consult Store Associates," Internet Retailer (December 6, 2010),

   http://www.internetretailer.com/2010/12/06/shoppers-would-rather-use
   -smartphones-store-associates.

b.   Ibid.

c.   "Accenture: Use of Smartphones by Bargain-Hunting Consumers Is
   Changing the Customer-Retailer Relationship," TMC News (December
   9, 2010), http://www.tmcnet.com/usubmit/2010/12/09/5184155.htm.

d.   "Who Is the Mobile Shopper?" Nielsen (July 2, 2013), http://www
   .nielsen.com/us/en/newswire/2013/who-is-the-mobile-shopper-.html.

e.   Diana McHenry, "Retail TouchPoints: Nearly 50 Percent of Consumers
   Believe They Are More Informed Than Store Associates," *RetailWire*
   blog, January 4, 2013, http://www.retailwire.com/blog-post/8f3d97de
   -dded-4df2-8e0b-fbd629deb5cb/retail-touchpoints-nearly-50-percent-of
   -consumers-believe-they-are-more-informed-than-store-associates.

f.   T. J. McCue, "Bring Your Own Device: In 2013 There Will Be More
   Mobile Devices Than People on Earth," *Forbes*, April 11, 2013,
   http://www.forbes.com/sites/tjmccue/2013/04/11/bring-your-own-device
   -in-2013-there-will-be-more-mobile-devices-than-people-on-earth/.

Chapter 5

1.   Donald G. Dutton and Arthur P. Aron, "Some Evidence for Heightened
   Sexual Attraction Under Conditions of High Anxiety," *Journal of
   Personality and Social Psychology* 30, no. 4 (1974): 510–517.

2.   "Customer Loyalty Engagement Index: 2013 Customer Loyalty
   Engagement Winners," Brand Keys (2013), http://brandkeys.com
   /syndicated-studies/customer-loyalty-engagement-index/2013
   -customer-loyalty-winners/.

3.   Julie Zischke, personal interview with Jessie Yarrow, on June 22,
   2013.

4.   Christina Binkley, "More Brands Want You to Model Their Clothes,"
   Wall Street Journal, May 15, 2013, http://online.wsj.com/news/articles/SB1
   0001424127887324216004578483094260521704.

5.   David Erickson, "Consumers' Attitudes Regarding Brands'
   Social Media Responses July 2013 [CHART]," *e-Strategy Trends*
   (July 2013), http://trends.e-strategyblog.com/2013/07/29
   /consumers-attitudes-toward-brands-social-media-responses/13100.

6.   Amanda Nelson, "25 Content Marketing Stats to Jumpstart Your
   Efforts," Salesforce blog, June 7, 2013, http://blogs.salesforce.com
   /company/2013/06/content-marketing-stats.html.

7. Jason Dubroy, VP managing director, shopper marketing, DDB Canada, personal interview with Kit Yarrow, May 13, 2013.

8. Drew Neisser, CEO, Renegade, personal interview with Kit Yarrow, July 2, 2013.

9. Stewart A. Shapiro and Jesper H. Nielsen, "What the Blind Eye Sees: Incidental Change Detection as a Source of Perceptual Fluency," *Journal of Consumer Research* 39, no. 6 (April 2013): 1202–1218.

Chapter 5 Feature Box Source Notes

a. Karlene Lukovitz, "Fastest-Growing Brands Are 'Ideal-Driven,'" *Marketing Daily*, January 18, 2012, http://www.mediapost.com /publications/article/165965/fastest-growing-brands-are-ideal-driven .html.

b. John Gerzema, "Understanding the Spend Shift," *Forbes*, November 29, 2010, http://www.forbes.com/2010/11/29/recession-consumers-values -spend-shift-sentiment-shopping-sales-leadership.html.

c. "Social Customer Service Performance Report," Conversocial (June 2013), http://landing.conversocial.com/download-performance -report-june-2013.

d. "The Evolution of Shopping" (chart in "Online Shoppers Say Their Path to Purchase Is Becoming More Complex, Personal"), Marketing Charts (February 2013), http://www.marketingcharts.com/wp/interactive /online-shoppers-say-their-path-to-purchase-is-becoming-more-complex -personal-26828/.

Chapter 6

1. Desmond Wong, "A Collection of 101 Companies Rocking Social Media Marketing," HubSpot (May 27, 2013), http://cdn1.hubspot.com /hub/53/101-Companies-Rocking-Social-media-HubSpotv5.pdf.

2. Josh Constine, "Where the Ladies At? Pinterest. 2 Million Daily Facebook Users, 97% of Fans Are Women," TechCrunch (February 11, 2012), http://techcrunch.com/2012/02/11/pinterest-stats/.

3. "Social Media by Gender: Women Dominate Pinterest, Twitter, Men Dominate Reddit, YouTube (INFOGRAPHIC)," *Huffington Post*, June 21, 2012, http://www.huffingtonpost.com/2012/06/20/social-media-by -gender-women-pinterest-men-reddit-infographic_n_1613812.html.

4. Jason Dubroy, VP managing director, shopper marketing, DDB Canada, personal interview with Kit Yarrow, May 13, 2013.

5. "Americans Are Watching More Online Video Ads Than Ever Before," Marketing Charts (July 18, 2013), http://www.marketingcharts.com/wp /interactive/americans-are-watching-more-online-video-ads-than-ever -before-35154/.

6. "The Data Behind 5 Brands Using Instagram Video," Measured, Analyzed & Reported (Simply Measured blog), June 27, 2013, http://simplymeasured.com/blog/2013/06/27/the-data-behind-5-brands -using-instagram-video/.

7. Karl Greenberg, "Honda Does Personalized Vines for Summer," *Marketing Daily*, July 15, 2013, http://www.mediapost.com/publications/article /204496/.

8. Greg Berardi, founder and chief marketing strategist, Blue Marlin Partners, personal interview with Kit Yarrow, May 10, 2013.

9. Richard Mullins, "Mullins: Savvy Software Lets You Visualize Your Buys," *Tampa Tribune*, September 15, 2013, http://tbo.com/news/business /mullins-savvy-software-lets-you-visualize-your-buys-20130915/.

10. Michael McCarthy, "Latest Items on Harley-Davidson's Crowd-Sourcing List: The Actual Bikes," *Advertising Age*, September 13, 2013, http://adage.com/article/news/harley-davidson-crowd-sources-ideas -rushmore-bikes/244126/.

11. "American Eagle Outfitters Announces Social Media Photo Contest," Business Wire (October 18, 2011), http://www.businesswire.com/news /home/20111018006389/en/American-Eagle-Outfitters-Announces -Social-Media-Photo.

Chapter 6 Feature Box Source Notes

a. Stacy DeBroff, "Customer Service Goes Social," Mom Central Consulting blog, June 20, 2013, http://insightblog.momcentralconsulting .com/2013/06/custom-service-goes-social.html.

b. "Less Than 20% of SMB Websites Link to Social Presence, According to SMB DigitalScape," PR Newswire (April 16, 2012), http://www .prnewswire.com/news-releases/less-than-20-of-smb-websites-link-to -social-presence-according-to-smb-digitalscape-147592525.html.

c. "Experian Marketing Services Reveals 27% of Time Spent Online Is on Social Media Sites," Experian (April 16, 2013), http://press.experian.com/ United-States/Press-Release/experian-marketing-services-reveals-27 -percent-of-time-spent-online-is-on-social-networking.aspx.

d. "Socialogue: It Pays to Be Social!" Ipsos Open Thinking Exchange (January 29, 2013), http://www.ipsos-na.com/news-polls/pressrelease .aspx?id=5974.

e. Ian Tenenbaum, "Brands That Dominate with User-Generated Content," iMediaConnection (July 9, 2013), http://www.imediaconnection.com /content/34502.asp.

Chapter 7

1. Jayne O'Donnell, reporter, *USA Today*, personal interview with Kit Yarrow, July 6, 2013.

2. "Restaurants Reel in Customers with Retail," Retail Customer Experience (March 21, 2013), http://www.retailcustomerexperience.com /article/210177/Restaurants-reel-in-customers-with-retail.

Chapter 7 Feature Box Source Notes

a. E. J. Schultz, "How America Eats Today," *Advertising Age*, November 11, 2012, http://adage.com/article/news/marketers-adapt-rapidly-changing -world-american-eating/238222/.

b. Darrell Etherington, "Mobile Payment at U.S. Starbucks Locations Crosses 10% as More Stores Get Wireless Charging," Techcrunch, July 26, 2013, http://techcrunch.com/2013/07/26/mobile-payment-at-u-s -starbucks-locations-crosses-10-as-more-stores-get-wireless-charging/

Acknowledgments and Gratitude

I sign my notes to my husband (Russ Yarrow) "WLG," an abbreviation for "world's luckiest girl." While writing this book, I realized I was even luckier than I knew. Russ is a former newspaper editor, and his encouragement and suggestions on my work were invaluable. With or without the bonus of his great writing skills, I am grateful every day to be married to Russ. He is the finest man I've ever known.

My sister, Diana Dykstra, is my lifelong best friend. Her quiet strength, fierce protectiveness, and wacky sense of humor are part of what makes her the anchor in my life.

I'm grateful to my mother, Laura Faller, a former math teacher, for showing me the joy of learning. She has more interests, more enthusiasm, and more college degrees than any mother of her generation I've ever met.

Golden Gate University has been my employer and my second family since I was a twenty-nine-year-old doctoral student. I am indebted to a long list of coworkers for their friendship and support. I'm particularly grateful to my wise and wonderful dean, Paul Fouts, and to my colleague Tom Wooldridge, who give me the peace of mind of knowing that the Psychology Department was in good hands while I spent less time in the office to research and write this book. I'm grateful for the support of Cassandra Dilosa, one of the smartest, kindest women I know; the good-natured Frances Sadaya, who has kept me laughing and helped me manage the Psychology Department for over a decade; and Nancy Lagomarsino, who cheerfully managed some of the administrative aspects of writing this book. I am also grateful to President Dan Angel, Barbara Karlin, and John Fyfe. They are the strong leadership behind the success and strength of Golden Gate University, and I'm grateful for their continuous support and confidence in my research.

I had the great good fortune of working with a top-notch team at Jossey-Bass: Nina Kreiden, Michele Jones, John Maas, Adrian Morgan, and Genoveva Llosa. Jossey-Bass is blessed with the best public relations expert in the business, Amy Packard, and I'm thrilled to be working with her once again.

Brad Tuttle, my editor at *TIME*, is a genius writer. His patient editing has been a great gift to me and improved my writing skills. So without his knowing it, Brad also made a giant contribution to this book.

My super-smart stepdaughter, Jessie Yarrow, provided research assistance on this book, as did my former student Denis Minaev, who is also the 2012 Outstanding Graduate of Golden Gate University's Psychology Department. I am grateful not only for the work they did but also for the pleasure of working with both of them. Public relations pro extraordinaire, Serene Buckley, provided just the boost I needed to get through a hurdle at the start of this project. I'm also grateful to talented journalist Allyson Rees for her initial input.

David Kaplan of the *Houston Chronicle* was the first reporter to call on me for insights about consumer psychology. Since then—for more than a decade now—he has inspired me with his creative, insightful story ideas. Silvercar, for example, was one of his story ideas.

My *Gen BuY* coauthor, Jayne O'Donnell, has continued to be someone I admire. She contributed to this book, and I'm grateful for her friendship and support.

My web designer, Bryan Kring, is also a fantastic artist. I feel so fortunate to have his keen eye and artistry creating the visual representation of my work. He also provided the initial vision of this book jacket.

I am grateful for the love and encouragement of a host of good friends while I wrote this book. I'm particularly thankful for the support of Karen Berardi, Cindy Kasabian, Margie Shafer, Maureen Egan, Jessica Notini, Caran Colvin, Kiki Kusek, the McLaughlins, the Stensruds, Mary Manning, Mitch Marks, Marcia Smolens, and Richard Rubin.

I am grateful to the professionals in the field—people I hold in the highest regard—whom I interviewed for this book. Every one of them is busy, and I am humbled by and grateful for their contributions.

I could not have written this book without the many consumers who have allowed me into their homes and their hearts. I am fortunate to have a career that allows me to know and appreciate the lives of so many different people. Every interview is exciting to me, and I'm awed by strength, struggles, humor, and humanity of the people I interview.

The greatest inspiration of my professional life is the work of Nobel laureate Daniel Kahneman. Nearly everything in the field of consumer psychology has sprung from one of the many seeds that he planted, and certainly I can attribute my own interest in consumer psychology to his work. I remember clearly the first time I read one of his studies—my heart raced.

The other great inspiration for my work has been Paco Underhill. His research and writing sparked a broad-scale interest in understanding the science of shopping. I call him the godfather of consumer behavior—because he also has a good sense of humor. I heard Paco speak at the Commonwealth Club in 1999, and he's been an inspiration to me since.

About the Author

Kit Yarrow, PhD, is an award-winning consumer research psychologist, professor, consultant, and keynote speaker. Her home base is Golden Gate University, where she chairs the Psychology Department and is a jointly appointed professor of both psychology and marketing. Kit's unique ability to apply clinical psychology to the field of behavioral economics has won her four endowed research professorships and recognition as the 2012 Outstanding Scholar of Golden Gate University.

Kit shares her findings and analysis in her blogs and articles for *TIME* and *Psychology Today*. She is also the coauthor of *Gen BuY: How Tweens, Teens, and Twenty-Somethings Are Revolutionizing Retail* (Jossey-Bass, 2009). As a widely recognized authority on the psychology of consumers, and on Generation Y in particular, Kit is regularly quoted in a variety of media, including the *New York Times*, the *Wall Street Journal*, *Marketplace*, *USA Today*, and *Good Morning America*.

Kit lives in the San Francisco Bay Area with her husband, Russ Yarrow. For more information, please visit kityarrow.com.

Index